THE ESSENTIAL GUIDE TO

Investing in
Precious
Metals

How to begin, build and maintain
a properly diversified portfolio

David L. Ganz

www.APMEX.com

Published by

Krause Publications, a division of F+W Media, Inc.
700 East State Street • Iola, WI 54990-0001
715-445-2214 • 888-457-2873
www.krausebooks.com

To order books or other products call toll-free 1-800-258-0929
or visit us online at www.shopnumismaster.com

ISBN-13: 978-1-4402-2369-3
ISBN-10: 1-4402-2369-6

Cover and Interior Design by Jana Tappa
Edited by Debbie Bradley

Printed in the United States

Table of Contents

Dedication

To my mother, Beverlee Ganz (1924-2011), who a half century ago in 1960, encouraged a young numismatist to inquire about a worn, circulated 1906 Indian head cent found in pocket change, and then convinced him that Elmer's Glue on shirt cardboard wasn't necessarily the best method of long-term coin storage.

And to my wife, Kathy, who continues to encourage me to collect and write about a subject that, like her, I love dearly.

Beverlee Ganz, David L. Ganz and Kathy Ganz aboard Crystal Symphony traversing the Panama Canal, 2007.

Metal Values Used in this Book

Generally speaking, this book uses $1,500 as a rounded number when referring to gold and $35 to $45 an ounce when referring to silver. The market and the price of the precious metals are so volatile as to make it easier to use the generalized number than the specific. Where calculations are given, the actual numbers utilized are provided. Troy ounces are converted from grams on the ratio of 1:31.1035.

WEIGHT OF A COIN IN TROY OUNCES
Troy weight is easy to calculate once you get the basics. There are 31.1035 grams in a single troy ounce, and 12 troy ounces in a troy pound. If a gold coin like the British sovereign is involved, you take its gross weight in grams (7.5739773), multiply by its fineness (.9167 fine) and then divide by 31.10352

Foreword

My friend David Ganz has done what he does best in *The Essential Guide to Investing in Precious Metals* – take a complex concept, synthesize it, illustrate it, analyze it and make it comprehensible to anyone needing information on the

 subject he addresses. He chose a propitious time for a book on precious metals, for as this goes to press, they are trading at levels reminiscent only of a short time in 1979 and 1980.

Through most of our lifetimes, we have witnessed a roller coaster ride for these commodities, but whether at the heights or the depths, they have always been the subject of an interest and fascination which far exceeded the number of people who traded in them. Why? Certainly not for their utilitarian value. Yes, palladium and platinum have important uses in a number of industrial applications including automobiles, electronics, medical and dental equipment and even drugs. Silver was long a staple of the photographic process and despite the emergence of the digital alternative, it remains the most widely used precious metal – in areas as diverse as traditional ones like silverware and jewelry, or industrial ones such as electronics and high-tech parts and equipment, and even new age uses such as solar energy and water treatment. As for gold, entire books have been written on the unique properties making it suitable in so many diverse applications, from ocean deeps to outer space.

While interesting, none of this is why precious metals have captivated humanity, and why they have done so, especially in the case of gold, for nearly the entire expanse of recorded history. When the layman is asked to think of gold, his thoughts turn to jewelry and to the use most familiar to us, coins. As we say in the preface to *Gold Coins of the World*, it has been man's ultimate measure of economic value. For rarity, purity, luster, resistance to the elements and time, and for color and beauty, it has nary an equal. In times of trouble it has been a source of security when all else lay in ruin.

Palladium has only recently been used in coinage. Platinum has been used since the 19th century, and gold and silver, forever. The collector and investor of today, however, faces a different set of challenges than any of his predecessors. Precious metal coins are no longer used in circulation and their face value bears no relation to their metal content. They carry either a significant premium because of their collector's value, or, if they are mass-produced, a very small one. Nor do they have a role in backing monetary reserves or will never again.

This is a book to guide the reader through what can be a confusing and not well-marked minefield: Whether to buy bullion coins or collector coins? Legal tender ones or metal ingots? American or foreign? In small quantities or in bulk? And in what metal? The answer, of course, is one that only the reader can provide himself. How to methodically arrive at that answer is why this book is invaluable.

— Arthur L. Friedberg
President, Coin & Currency Institute,
May 2011

About the Author

David L. Ganz (b. 1951) has traveled the world and had a multi-faceted career. He authored *A Beginner's Guide to Better Coins* in 1965, the same year he started writing the monthly column "Under the Glass" for *The Coin Shopper.* He began writing a column with the same name for *The Coin Collector,* published by the Lawrence Brothers of Anamosa, IA., in 1967, the same year he joined the American Numismatic Association. By 1969, he moved the column to *Numismatic News,* changed its frequency and became the paper's Washington Correspondent (1969-1973).

From that vantage point, he covered the battle in Congress to restore the right for Americans to own gold, witnessed the Hobby Protection Act creation, reported on the legislation that evolved into America's bicentennial coins and other laws passed by Congress. A graduate of Georgetown University's School of Foreign Service with a B.S. in Foreign Service, he received his law degree from St. John's University Law School in 1976. The following year, he wrote the seminal law review article "Toward a Revision of the Minting & Coinage Laws of the United States" which appeared in volume 26 of the *Cleveland State Law Review* 175-257 (1977), and was reprinted in its entirety in *The Numismatist.* Many of the suggested revisions have since been individually enacted by Congress.

He has written more than 30 books on a variety of subjects (from "A" [for *A Critical Guide to Anthologies of African Literature*] to "Z" [*Zoning Law*], and a number of coin books, recently including *The Smithsonian Guide to Coin Collecting* (2008), *Profitable Coin Collecting* (2008), *Rare Coin Investing* (2010), and *America's State Quarters* (2008).

In 1974, President Nixon appointed him to the U.S. Assay Commission, and later that year, as a journalist, he testified before the House consumer affairs subcommittee on coinage matters, the first of more than a dozen times since that he has addressed Congress on gold, silver and other coinage matters. In the fall of 1974, he was invited on the Congressional inspection trip to Fort Knox, and is now one of the "last standing" who have visited and taken floor tours of all U.S. Mints and bullion depositories. Over the past quarter century, he has also been a contributing editor to *Gold Coins of the World* by Arthur L. Friedberg and Ira Friedberg and served as a consultant to several precious-metal based international coin programs.

After serving on various committees of the American Numismatic Association from 1969 to 1984, and acting as the organization's legislative counsel, he was elected to the ANA Board (1985) and served for a decade, culminating with his becoming 48th President (1993-1995). Treasury Secretary Lloyd Bentsen designated him as a charter member of the Citizens Commemorative Coin Advisory Committee, and it was in that capacity that he became a critical advocate for the State quarters program that has brought over 130 million Americans to collecting these distinctive numismatic items. He served as mayor of Fair Lawn N.J., for seven years, and was recently re-elected to a fourth three-year term as Bergen County Freeholder (a county supervisor).

When he's not doing all of this coin and political stuff, he has practiced law in New York City for more than 30 years as senior partner in Ganz & Hollinger, P.C. He has three adult children and resides in Fair Lawn, N.J., with his wife Kathy and their four felines.

About APMEX

APMEX is one of the world's largest Internet-based precious metals retailers, offering competitively priced Gold, Silver, Platinum and Palladium products 24-hours a day, 7-days-a-week on its website at www.APMEX.com.

Individual investors, families, individual collectors, investment advisors, family trusts, investment funds and other individual investors from around the world come to APMEX for precious metals assets and related depository services. In addition to convenient web access, APMEX assists customers through dedicated telephone representatives trained in asset allocation and investment diversification. Phone support is available at 1-800-375-9006.

APMEX stocks a broad range of precious metals products, with over 3,500 different items in both coin and bar form, including products from sovereign governments. The company carries:

- All U.S. Mint bullion products (including gold, silver and platinum American Eagles)
- All Royal Canadian Mint products (such as gold, silver and platinum Maple Leafs and bars)
- A wide selection of semi-numismatic and numismatic collectible coins
- Supplies to help protect and display bullion coins, bars and coin collections

APMEX continuously updates buy and sell prices on the website to ensure transparency and full disclosure.

In addition, an APMEX subsidiary, Citadel Global Depository Services, provides maximum security of precious metals through an exclusive partnership with a global leader in security-related vaulting services. APMEX also helps long-term investors take advantage of precious metals individual retirement accounts (IRAs), by working with IRA administrators and precious metals depositories.

Finally, APMEX provides useful research, information and education through daily commentaries and weekly market reports. Registration is free on the website at www.APMEX.com.

www.APMEX.com

"A ONCE IN TWO OR

THREE GENERATION

OPPORTUNITY TO

NOT ONLY OBSERVE

PRECIOUS METALS

MARKETS, BUT TO BE

THE MARKET...."

A Precious Metal Moment

This is a precious moment in time – a precious metal moment. Psychological and market barriers of yesteryear have been breached. The United States and other major economic countries have virtually unsustainable government debt. Gold market highs of 1980 have been swept aside. The year 2011 was filled with milestones.

Gold first pushed past $1,500 an ounce, then went to $1,900 before beginning a gyration. Silver moved above $30, then $40, retreated to $30 an ounce and threw smelters into a tizzy. Platinum switched with gold for top dog, and the Dow Jones Industrial Average (DJIA) swung like a Duncan yo-yo.

Multiple vintage U.S. gold coins.

American inflation was under control, the U.S. dollar was under attack, foreign currencies were in their ascendancy and coins, including bullion and trade coins, were in their heyday.

Using prices in here may suggest to you that this book will be dated in another year. Nonsense. It is part of history, and if you are buying and selling precious metals, you are a part of it. That is exciting – a once in two or three generation opportunity to not only observe precious metals markets, but to *be* the market, or at least a component in it.

If you are serious about precious metal investing, you will need to see

INDEXED PERFORMANCE OR PRECIOUS METALS AND THE DOW JONES INDUSTRIAL AVERAGE (1970 = 100)

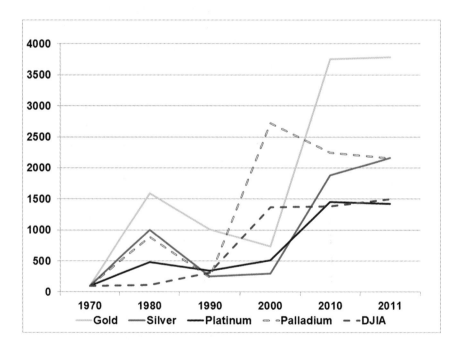

the numbers, watch the market go up and down, and memorize some of the formulas and decide what to put your money into. You could:

- Buy bullion product such as ingots and bars.
- Buy bullion coins such as the American Eagle, Canadian Maple Leaf or South African Krugerrand.
- Acquire semi-numismatic precious metals coins such as pre-1933 U.S. gold coins or pre-1921 U.S. silver dollars
- Acquire numismatic precious metal coins in superior condition (generally encapsulated)
- Buy stock or certificates in a gold-acquiring company.
- Buy certificates or warehouse receipts for gold.
- Acquire gold coins in MS-60 or MS-61 condition (a little more expensive than a pure bullion purchase, but good value).
- A combination of many variations on this approach.

My suggestion: use this book as your reference point to help you through the analysis that you have to do every time you want to buy or sell.

It is an exciting time for anyone who has followed the precious metals market for the last half century. Gold is behaving in a manner that does not correspond with prior performance. Silver is not being squeezed, but has catapulted in value.

Gold coins that in the 1930s and before had virtually the same value as the denomination stamped on their face or reverse now have a worth that is substantially more. A U.S. $20 gold piece (which once had $19.99 in gold) now multiplies 0.9675 troy ounces by the daily price of gold on the London spot market and finds its metal worth over $1,500 – before adding any numismatic value.

What's true for gold is even more so for silver: even the simple 1942-45 War nickel (with .05626 troy ounces of silver) is worth just about $2 as silver crosses the $35 an ounce mark.

There are now precious metal legal tender coins struck by the U.S. Mint at the direction of Congress (which encouraged gold ownership through their legislation) that include gold, silver, platinum and, starting in 2011, palladium. Since 1985, the U.S. Mint has sold over 250 million ounces of silver to the public. Gold total sales are around 24 million ounces. At current market prices, that's over $11 billion in silver and more than $36 billion in gold.

Why the current interest in gold, silver and precious metals? In this book, I will provide information to help you understand and comprehend both the current and historical elements of gold, silver and precious metals as both an investment and a monetary instrument.

As the calendar turned to the year 2000, it appears that a new age also dawned on investments. The "lost decade" of the stock market up to 2010 is more than just a play on words. Almost every investor in America saw their portfolios stagnate or drop up to 50% as the S&P 500 (one of the broadest indicators of stock prices in the U.S.) failed to significantly improve during the decade. However, as you can see from graph below, gold held its value or increased during the same period while the U.S. debt significantly increased

---

INDEXED COMPARISON OF THE S&P 500, GOLD, U.S. DEBT, AND U.S. GROSS DOMESTIC PRODUCT (GDP) 2000 = 100

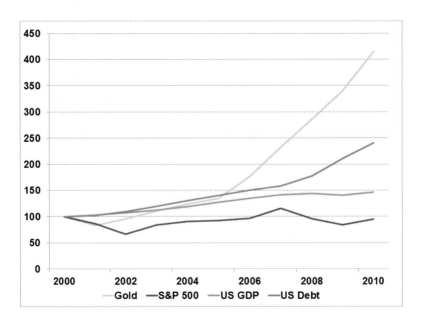

and the U.S. Gross Domestic Product (GDP) did not keep up with the increase in the debt.

The negative correlation between the historical results of the S&P 500 and gold (the two indices seem to move in opposite directions during the same time frame) is an important concept to recall as we continue to review precious metals as a part of a diversified portfolio.

In the early 1950s, Harry Markowitz wrote a thesis on portfolio theory which proved mathematically, among other theories, that a portfolio with an allocation among asset groups showed increased performance over other investment methods. Markowitz won the Nobel Prize in Economics and the book, *Modern Portfolio Theory*, laid a foundation for decades to come for financial advisors to follow.

Unfortunately, during the severe financial crisis in the U.S. in 2008 (and which seems to continue), portfolio allocation among cash, stocks and bonds did not provide balance as these asset classes moved generally in the same direction in a relative high, positive correlation. Was Markowitz wrong in his prize winning theory? No, the mathematics are correct, rather it was the asset classes that may have been wrong. If an investor had included gold as an asset class along with cash, stocks and bonds during the "lost decade," the performance of the entire portfolio would have improved proportionately with the allocation of gold.

Therefore, one could conclude that a balanced portfolio is one that includes asset classes that are not all positively correlated, but rather, some of the asset classes must have a negative correlation to other asset classes. With some asset classes in positive asset correlation and some asset classes in negative correlation, the Markowitz prize winning theory begins to take effect and the entire portfolio begins to improve in performance.

What is that asset class that can be added to cash, stocks and bonds to provide the negative correlation? If history is our guide, then gold, silver and precious metals would be that fourth asset class.

There is little doubt that today the American people are waking up to the imbalance in their portfolios and have begun to vote with their wallets making this the precious metals moment in this decade by adding gold, silver and precious metals as the fourth asset class.

"DO YOU BELIEVE THAT GOLD COINS ARE EXPENSIVE? WELL, YOU'RE ABOUT TO FIND OUT HOW GOLD CAN BE PART OF YOUR INVESTMENT STRATEGY AT A VARIETY OF PRICE POINTS."

CHAPTER 1

Keys to the Precious Metals Market

I. Buying and selling precious metals

Buying and selling precious metals – gold, silver, platinum and palladium – can be fun and profitable. It can be a lucrative investment, a way to plan for your golden years of retirement with real gold.

There are also other opportunities to extend your interest into "rare and unusual" coins. You can buy bullion legal tender coinage, or bars of silver, platinum, palladium and gold in a variety of sizes, weights, designs, and packaging.

*One Ounce
Silver Bars from
APMEX*

LEGAL TENDER: IT IS WHAT IT IS

Legal tender is simply a law of compulsion.

First used in China, Marco Polo described how the Chinese emperor required his subjects to accept paper money on pain of death. That incentive compelled them to comply.

Our coinage laws initially made all coin a legal tender with limitations. For instance, cents are legal tender to 25 cents. That is, you can't force someone to take more than 25 cents in change or payment. Dimes, quarters and half dollars were traditionally legal tender up to $10.

An 1877-S Trade Dollar

Originally, gold was legal tender for its fully declared value, weight, and measure. Today, precious metal coinage has a nominal legal tender value declared and usually stated on the coin. It could be a silver dollar with legal tender value of $1, a commemorative coin with a legal tender value of $5 or a bullion item like the 5-ounce silver America the Beautiful coin with a legal tender value of 25 cents.

The "legal tender" value is simply an accounting device. It bears no reality to the cost of production, the metal in the coin, or anything other than what the Mint recommended, or the legislature demanded.

Legal tender does mean, for example, that you can take a platinum $50 bullion coin worth around $700 on the open market, and go to the post office and demand $50 worth of postage stamps.

Or you can do what I did a few years ago when I took an old 1877-S Trade dollar in Very Fine condition with a legal tender value of $1 and asked the Mint to exchange it for a new Presidential dollar. The Trade dollar was valued on the open market at $175, while the Presidential dollar was worth $1.

But the Mint did the exchange at Grand Central Station terminal in New York City, even though the staff cautioned me that the older coin was worth "a lot more."

2. Gold coins aren't always expensive

Do you believe that gold coins are expensive? Well, you're about to find out how gold can be part of your investment strategy at a variety of price points.

A 1/10 ounce $5 gold coin

Although silver may be more in your price range at about $40 an ounce, don't think gold is out of your reach. An investor can acquire a fractional portion of an ounce of gold in coin form, ingot form, or even a physical paper share, which is like a shareholder with stock in a company. A 1/10 ounce gold American Eagle coin can be purchased for under $200 when gold is trading at about $1,600 an ounce.

3. Silver the early favorite for coins

Silver's history is as fascinating as gold's. Silver is a metal that our Founding Fathers insisted on using in our coinage, but America had no native silver mines. Coin production depended on private individuals bringing silver to the Mint, mostly Spanish coins that were then melted.

A silver peso

Silver was the metal of choice for much of the world's coins until 1965 when the price jumped above $1.29 an ounce. That allowed U.S. coinage, and that of many other countries, to be melted for its precious metal content. After that, silver became a significant investment vehicle in the form of medallions, ingots, flatware and bags of U.S. silver coins.

4. Platinum and palladium join the group

Two other precious metals are platinum and palladium, which are from the platinum family of metals. They are rare metals and were not known to the ancients. Today they join gold and silver as

A platinum coin from Australia

the basis for the U.S. Mint precious
metals coin and bullion program.

A Canadian palladium coin

Palladium coinage was directed
by Congress to begin in 2011, and
soon it will join platinum as another
great metal that has some commercial
potential.

There is considerably less platinum
and palladium available than there
is gold and silver, and the market
is more volatile. Although there
are many platinum and palladium bullion coins and products (ingots,
bars, rounds and so forth), the number of coins originally intended for
circulation are few and the number of collector-oriented items many.

5. U.S. Mint promotes precious metal sales

Selling bullion, bars, ingots,
coins and medallions made of
these precious metals is big
business for the U.S. Mint, which
began the modern era of precious
metals sales in 1986. Since
then, the U.S. Mint, backed by a
network of dealers, has sold more
than 250 million ounces of silver,
24 million ounces of gold, and
about a half million ounces of
platinum.

A 5 ounce silver bullion coin from the U.S. Mint

Valued at today's market, silver
sales top $7.4 billion, aggregate gold
sales are at $38.8 billion and platinum totals $984 million. All told, that
comes in $46 billion worth of metals sold by the U.S. Mint.

6. Government holdings of gold

Yes, Virginia, there is gold in Fort Knox. In fact, the United States is the world leader in gold holdings with over 8,965 metric tons or about 261 million troy ounces. Value: $483 billion. And truly, a nation or governmental entity that controls that much gold has a say at the table over its future, but it's not enough to influence the gold market as a whole.

Thirteen nations and two international organizations, The International Monetary Fund and the European Central Bank, have about 26,307 metric tons of gold in their holdings. That's $1.56 trillion when valued at about $1,600 a troy ounce.

The United States currently has about 30.9% of the world's gold reserves. If you add the next three nations with the largest reserves (Germany with 3,400 tons, Italy with 2,450 tons and France with 2,400 tons), they don't quite equal the American hoard.

The American economy, however, depends not on how much gold it holds, but what it produces and what it can buy in the marketplace. The dollar is not convertible by the holder to gold; it is usable to purchase goods and services. And the United States still produces a lot more of these than other nations.

7. Bullion, numismatic coins marry

A price analysis of the gold, silver, platinum and palladium market for bullion coins shows that immediately after minting, bullion coins have value because of their metal content only. However, as time passes, many of the bullion coins become collectible as the specific dates of years past are desired by collectors who wish to build a set with one coin from each year. These older year bullion coins are bid up in the marketplace to include premiums in excess of the metal content, with aggregate value representing a collectible or numismatic value.

Many of today's numismatic or collectible rarities began their lives as bullion coins. In fact, some of the great numismatic collections were built buying gold coins for little more than their bullion value.

Legendary coin collectors John Jay Pittman, Louis Eliasberg and Harold Bareford all took advantage of this.

8. Precious metals now!

Precious metals have an imprecise definition, and may change over time, but they nonetheless have a number of commonalities. Here are some general traits:

- Rare or scarce.
- Available in limited quantity
- Chemically less reactive than other elements
- High luster
- More ductile than other metals
- Higher melting points
- Historically used as currency
- Traded in commodity markets
- May have a value that increases and decreases over time.
- Display good tensile strength and conductivity
- Price reflects scarcity or rarity but may vary

9. An example of my precious metal retirement

Back in 1998, I decided to buy $10,000 worth of "rare coins" and turn them into a retirement plan. The coins were all "rare coins," but none were terribly expensive. Because it is the best known and most followed precious metal, a secondary portfolio was also devised consisting of gold coins that would legally be called "rare and unusual," but also inexpensive. None cost over an average of about $100 each.

There were 103 gold coins in that portfolio. The gold coins came from 54 countries or issuing authorities (the United States is a country; a ducat dated 1789 from Venice, Italy, is from an issuing authority). The average cost of the 103 coins was $85.73; the total weight of all 103 coins was a shade over 17 ounces (12 troy ounces of gold equals a troy pound) and the average weight of each gold coin was about 0.16 troy ounces (which at $303 an ounce, the average price in 1998 would have meant that there was a core melt value of the coins of about $5,100).

Today, when evaluating the 1998 portfolio strictly on the basis of the precious metal content, the results are startling. Gold is a product that shows to be a bona fide investment. Here is the growth from 1998 to 2011.

- 103 gold coins (same as 1998)
- 17.09 troy ounces – weight of gold coin portfolio
- $1,625/troy ounce – market price of gold
- $27,776.43 – value of metal in the 103 coins
- $18,774.25 – profit on the portfolio
- 9.8% – annual rate of return compounded over 12 years
- 2.75% – Dow increase compounded 1998-2011
- 2.5% – rate by which gold outpaces the Consumer Price Index, 1998-2011

From this, it is clear that gold is in the catbird seat.

10. Owning precious metals: the choices

You can buy or acquire precious metal in many different forms.

In Table 1, starting on page 26, are the prices and premiums for various bullion coin products on a random date, March 18, 2011: The London Fix on each of the principal precious metals was:

- Gold $1,420
- Silver $35.15
- Platinum $1,720
- Palladium $720

11. A word about pricing

Historical pricing in the precious metals field may be confusing, especially for gold. That's because there is a "free market" price set by negotiation between business parties, and an "official" price at which world governments value the gold held in their reserves.

From the mid-1830s until 1933, gold was officially priced at $20.67 an ounce – the same price it held in the marketplace. Then, in 1933, President Franklin Roosevelt

FIXED VALUE OF A SILVER DOLLAR

Weight .7734 troy ounce multiplied by the price of silver.
At $10 an ounce: $7.73
At $20 an ounce: $15.46
At $30 an ounce: $23.20
At $40 an ounce: $30.94

devalued the dollar by raising the official price of gold to $35 an ounce. The

TABLE 1: MODERN ISSUES CURRENTLY BEING SOLD WITH PREMIUM COST COMPARISON.

	Price of Metal*	Premium	Total Cost	% Premium
90% Silver Coins - $100 Face Value	$ 2,552.00	$ 58.63	$ 2,610.63	2.30%
90% Silver Coins - $1,000 Face Value	$ 25,520.14	$ 514.50	$ 26,034.64	2.02%
Gold - 1 oz Chinese Panda Coin .999	$ 1,417.50	$ 77.04	$ 1,494.54	5.43%
Gold - 100 g cast bar	$ 1,417.50	$ 59.29	$ 1,476.79	4.18%
Gold - 100 g Minted Bar .9999	$ 1,417.50	$ 59.29	$ 1,476.79	4.18%
Gold 10 oz Cast Bar Johnson Matthey	$ 1,417.50	$ 59.29	$ 1,476.79	4.18%
Gold Bar 1 oz	$ 1,417.50	$ 31.00	$ 1,448.50	2.19%
Gold Bar 1 oz Perth Mint	$ 1,417.50	$ 58.63	$ 1,476.13	4.14%
Gold Bar 10 oz Perth Mint	$ 1,417.50	$ 58.63	$ 1,476.13	4.14%
Gold Bar 5 oz	$ 1,417.50	$ 58.63	$ 1,476.13	4.14%
Gold Buffalo 1 oz	$ 1,417.50	$ 58.63	$ 1,476.13	4.14%
Gold Eagle 1 oz	$ 1,417.50	$ 58.63	$ 1,476.13	4.14%
Gold Eagle 1/10 oz	$ 141.75	$ 58.63	$ 200.38	41.36%
Gold Eagle ½ oz	$ 708.75	$ 58.63	$ 767.38	8.27%
Gold Eagle 1/4 oz	$ 354.38	$ 58.63	$ 413.01	16.54%

TABLE 1: MODERN ISSUES CURRENTLY BEING SOLD WITH PREMIUM COST COMPARISON.

	Price of Metal*	Premium	Total Cost	% Premium
Gold Krugerrand 1 oz	$ 1,417.50	$ 58.63	$ 1,476.13	4.14%
Gold Maple 1 oz	$ 1,417.50	$ 58.63	$ 1,476.13	4.14%
Gold Maple 1/10 oz	$ 141.75	$ 58.63	$ 200.38	41.36%
Gold Maple ½ oz	$ 708.75	$ 58.63	$ 767.38	8.27%
Gold Maple 1/20 oz	$ 70.88	$ 58.63	$ 129.51	82.72%
Gold Maple 1/4 oz	$ 354.38	$ 58.63	$ 413.01	16.54%
Gold Philharmonic 1 oz	$ 1,417.50	$ 58.63	$ 1,476.13	4.14%
Gold Philharmonic 20 oz	$ 28,350.00	$ 58.63	$ 28,408.63	0.21%
Kitco 500 oz Cast Silver Bar	$ 17,640.00	$ 410.00	$ 18,050.00	2.32%
Olympic Gold Maple 1 oz 2008	$ 1,417.50	$ 58.63	$ 1,476.13	4.14%
Olympic Gold Maple 1 oz 2009	$ 1,417.50	$ 58.63	$ 1,476.13	4.14%
Olympic Gold Maple 1 oz 2010	$ 1,417.50	$ 58.63	$ 1,476.13	4.14%
Olympic Silver Maple 1 oz 2008	$ 35.28	$ 4.22	$ 39.50	11.96%
Olympic Silver Maple 1 oz 2009	$ 35.28	$ 4.22	$ 39.50	11.96%
Olympic Silver Maple 1 oz 2010	$ 35.28	$ 4.22	$ 39.50	11.96%

TABLE 1: MODERN ISSUES CURRENTLY BEING SOLD WITH PREMIUM COST COMPARISON.

	Price of Metal*	Premium	Total Cost	% Premium
Palladium Bar 1 oz	$ 729.00	$ 40.00	$ 769.00	5.49%
Palladium Bar 1000 g	$ 23,437.35	$ 1,189.00	$ 24,626.35	5.07%
Palladium Maple 1 oz	$ 729.00	$ 55.00	$ 784.00	7.54%
Platinum Bar 1 oz	$ 1,721.00	$ 83.00	$ 1,804.00	4.82%
Platinum Bar 10 oz	$ 17,210.00	$ 580.00	$ 17,790.00	3.37%
Platinum Eagle 1 oz	$ 1,721.00	$ 156.42	$ 1,877.42	9.09%
Platinum Eagle 1/10 oz	$ 172.10	$ 22.55	$ 194.65	13.10%
Platinum Eagle ½ oz	$ 860.50	$ 86.21	$ 946.71	10.02%
Platinum Eagle 1/4 oz	$ 430.25	$ 47.73	$ 477.98	11.09%
Platinum Koala 1 oz	$ 1,721.00	$ 156.32	$ 1,877.32	9.08%
Platinum Maple 1 oz	$ 1,721.00	$ 156.32	$ 1,877.32	9.08%
Platinum Noble 1 oz	$ 1,721.00	$ 156.32	$ 1,877.32	9.08%
Silver Bar 10 oz	$ 352.80	$ 19.20	$ 372.00	5.44%
Silver Bar 100 oz	$ 3,528.00	$ 162.00	$ 3,690.00	4.59%
Silver Bar 100 oz RCM Minted	$ 3,528.00	$ 162.00	$ 3,690.00	4.59%
Silver Bar 1000 oz	$ 35,280.00	$ 670.00	$ 35,950.00	1.90%

TABLE 1: MODERN ISSUES CURRENTLY BEING SOLD WITH PREMIUM COST COMPARISON.

	Price of Metal*	Premium	Total Cost	% Premium
Silver Grizzly Bear 1oz	$ 35.28	$ 6.22	$ 41.50	17.63%
Silver Koala 1 Kg	$ 1,134.25	$ 95.49	$ 1,229.74	8.42%
Silver Koala 1 oz	$ 35.28	$ 4.47	$ 39.75	12.67%
Silver Koala 10 oz	$ 352.80	$ 24.20	$ 377.00	6.86%
Silver Kookaburra 1 Kg	$ 1,134.25	$ 95.49	$ 1,229.74	8.42%
Silver Kookaburra 1 oz	$ 35.28	$ 4.47	$ 39.75	12.67%
Silver Kookaburra 10 oz	$ 352.80	$ 95.49	$ 448.29	27.07%
Silver Lunar 1 Kg	$ 1,134.25	$ 95.49	$ 1,229.74	8.42%
Silver Lunar 1 oz	$ 35.28	$ 4.47	$ 39.75	12.67%
Silver Lunar 10 oz	$ 352.80	$ 25.28	$ 378.08	7.17%
Silver Maple 1 oz	$ 35.28	$ 4.22	$ 39.50	11.96%
Silver RCM Wolf Coin 1 oz 2011	$ 35.28	$ 4.97	$ 40.25	14.09%
Special Gold Maple 5 X 9 pure 1 oz	$ 1,417.00	$ 91.24	$ 1,508.24	6.44%
			AVERAGE=>	9.75%

market price and official price remained more or less the same until 1968, when a two-tiered market (official and unofficial) price began.

It reached its apogee on Jan. 16, 1970, when the official price was $35 an ounce and the free market price fell slightly to $34.90. Since then, it has been a march of progress. Today, the official price of gold is at $42.22 an ounce, while the free market price is some 40 times higher.

This "book price" is what is found in the Treasury Department's balance sheet statement, which is why so many people have a practical difficulty in understanding how bullion coins of today compare with older numismatic coins that once circulated.

Melt value, by contrast, is what the precious metal coin would bring if it were put into the melting cauldron, devoid of manufacturing or distribution costs or any numismatic value. Melt price is what the refinery pays.

But just because the market value of gold is $1,680 doesn't mean the refinery will pay $1,680 for a 1 ounce gold coin. Everybody has to make some money, and the refinery has costs to melt, refine, redistribute and finance the gold in order to bring the gold back to the market.

Today, gold will be priced differently depending on the form of delivery. The differences in price relate directly to the manufacturing, distribution and marketing costs for the issuer. All of these costs are added to the current market price, or spot value, of the gold as a premium.

Gold in bar form carries the lowest costs of conversion and accordingly the lowest premium in excess of the gold spot value. Gold in coin form, as issued by a sovereign government, carries a higher cost of conversion because of the minting cost, and often includes a guarantee of purity and authenticity by the issuing government.

So, with a hypothetical gold 1 ounce bullion coin, here's how the value might look with gold quoted at $1,638 an ounce.

LONDON FIX	$1,638	RETAIL PRICE		BUY-BACK PRICE	
Spot Market	$1,619	Maple Leaf	$1,651	Maple Leaf	$1,611
Melt value	$1,604	1 oz Bar	$1,641	1 oz. Bar	$1,601
Melt price	$1,551	U.S. Eagle	$1,673	U.S. Eagle	$1,631
Official Price	$42.22	Krugerrand	$1,651	Krugerrand	$1,611

There are a number of other prices for buy and sell transactions involving many different sizes, weights and denominations for gold, silver, platinum and palladium. For up-to-date prices, check out the APMEX website, www.APMEX.com.

12. How much precious metal to buy

While the asset allocation in your portfolio is a matter best determined by you to meet your investment objectives, there are certain factors you should consider in your decision.

Just like reviewing your asset allocation in your IRA, 401(k) or other portfolio, your objectives include many considerations, but most likely include the following: (a) analysis of preservation of your investment capital, (b) the "real" return on your investments as a whole ("real" return is the nominal return or the actual return, less inflation over the investment period), (c) your investment period (short term – less than one year, intermediate term – three to five years, long term – more than five years), (d) liquidity (how fast you can turn your investments into cash), (e) your tolerance for risk and uncertainty over the investment period and other considerations.

Generally, a balanced portfolio is one that has both positive and negative correlations among the asset classes. Of course, no asset class always increases every year, but one of the keys to a balanced portfolio is to initiate, maintain and change the allocation between asset classes so that for the time and the season of the investment cycles, you move fund allocation between asset classes, some increasing and some decreasing, based on your view of the economic future. Some of the asset classes tend to move together under certain economic conditions (a positive correlation) and some asset classes tend to move opposite other asset classes (a negative correlation). The concept of a balanced portfolio is to always have some allocation in all asset classes (since it is impossible to correctly predict the economic future) and you balance or re-balance among the asset classes based on your own view of the economic future. This strategy does not yield a real return on every asset class (because of the negative correlation among the classes) but the objective is to have the real returns more than offset the real losses so that the capital is preserved, as well as to provide a net real return on the entire portfolio.

1884-S Morgan dollar

Most investors consider the asset classes to be cash, stocks, bonds and the fourth asset class of alternatives or tangible assets. One of the largest assets in the fourth asset class is gold and precious metals and this class has historically held a negative correlation to cash, stocks and bonds. While there are negative correlations among cash, stocks and bonds, there are certain economies when these three asset classes move together (or positively correlate) and without the fourth asset class of gold and precious metals, under those economic conditions your portfolio will be out of balance and you may experience net real losses on your entire portfolio resulting in the loss of your investment capital. Perhaps your portfolio experienced a loss of capital during the U.S. economic crisis of 2008 as all of your allocated asset classes were correlated and all did not provide a real return.

The allocation among the asset classes of cash, stocks, bonds and the fourth asset class of gold and precious metals is one of the most important strategic decisions you will make about your portfolio. My purpose in this book is to assist you in understanding the fourth asset class of gold and precious metals so you can allocate properly for your investments.

Here is a final thought on asset allocation: mathematically, an asset allocation of less than 5% of the total assets most likely will not significantly balance the portfolio. Consider the possible results of this economic scene: if the correlated assets are 99% of the portfolio and the economic conditions are such that the correlated assets do not provide a real return, for example declining in value by 20%, even if the 1% allocation of non-correlated assets increase by 100%, the results are as follows: (1) correlated asset original allocation 97% of portfolio value, after real losses, 79% of original portfolio value; (2) non-correlated asset original allocation 3%, after real returns, 6% of original portfolio value; (3) aggregate of original value after this allocation, 85% of original portfolio value. You can easily work through a variety of scenarios for your own asset allocation among cash, stocks and bonds (sometimes highly correlated) and the fourth asset class gold and precious metals (sometimes highly non-correlated).

13. How to buy precious metals

When buying precious metal bullion coins or products, there are a number of ways that an investor can conclude the transaction. Here are several ways:

- Take physical possession and delivery immediately upon payment.
- Buy it and enter into a storage arrangement with the vendor or third party with ownership in your name.
- Enter into a payment arrangement with the vendor maintaining possession until payment is made in full.
- Make arrangements with an independent warehouse to manage the purchase.
- Leave the purchase with the dealer so the bullion can be easily traded or transferred.
- Buy the equivalent of a "warehouse receipt" where the precious metal is not specifically identified or segregated.
- Buy the equivalent of a "warehouse receipt" where the precious metal is specifically identified or segregated.
- Always obtain a written receipt detailing any coins or bullion purchased.

At one time, the coins of the United States were made of precious metal and the face value of the coins were equal to the value of the precious metals content. What you saw was what you got. Between 1849 and 1933, a gold double eagle with a face value of $20 contained $20 worth of gold (0.9675 troy ounces). And from 1794 to 1965, a silver dollar weighing a little over 3/4 ounce (.7734 troy ounces) contained a dollar's worth of silver.

14. Where to buy precious metals

There are generally three ways to buy precious metals: (1) purchase from a retail establishment in your local geography; (2) purchase from a telemarketer; and (3) purchase online from an Internet retailer. For a more specific review of the differences in each of these buying channels, please see Chapter 14.

For perhaps the last 2,000 years, gold and silver have been available at retail sellers in what is basically an over-the-counter retail presentation. Today, gold and precious metals are available in the U.S. at almost every one of the approximately 10,000 local coin dealers while in Europe and Asia, gold and precious metals are also available at some bank branches. Generally, the local coin dealers are individually owned and operated stores in strip malls and other retail locations and along with the gold and precious metals, offer rare and collectible coins and possibly rare stamps and other collectibles. Because the local coin dealer serves an area and population that is geographically limited, the local coin dealer has a limit on the total annual sales volume and accordingly, maintains inventory and availability only meet that limited demand.

Telemarketing retail began in the 1960s and later years as 1-800 inbound telephone service was developed along with lower and competitive outbound long distance rates. In the U.S., a very few coin dealers seized upon this opportunity and initiated telemarketing businesses in the late 1980s and 1990s, taking advantage of a national market and geography so that annual sales had the potential to be much larger than the local coin dealer model and as a result, larger selections and availability was improved. Over time, the telemarketing model has changed and today there are a few national retailers with telemarketing services.

With the advent of the Internet in the 21st century, almost all retailers started adding an Internet component to the local bricks and mortar businesses. A few Internet retailers have developed over the last 10 years that have taken full advantage of the lower cost model of one central inventory that is wide, extensive and immediately available, lower cost of order taking and processing and provided the customer with 24/7/365 access to buying.

In the U.S. markets, a few retailers have established very large businesses by providing the added convenience and lower cost of the Internet distribution model. In the gold and precious metals markets in the U.S., just like in other retail markets, there are very few large and successful Internet retailers. Purchasing from a large, Internet retailer like APMEX at www.APMEX.com, offers perhaps the best selection for immediate delivery with the convenience of web-based ordering system which does not require (but is at your option) talking to what is often a commission-based salesman either at a local coin dealer or at a national telemarketer.

"So how do you determine if a coin is considered numismatic (collectible) or bullion?"

CHAPTER 2

Bullion Prices Always Change

This is a book about bullion, bullion coinage, and bullion-like coinage. And it's also about the fluctuating value of precious metals and the price of the bullion item to be purchased.

Just for the record, gold and silver are today the same gold and silver that has been used in commerce for more than 2,000 years. Gold is often called a currency without a country and the fact that today's currencies fluctuate in value relative to, for example, one ounce of gold or silver demonstrates not the movement of gold, but rather the change in the value of the currency of the issuing country. Currencies of countries change relative to one another and relative to gold and silver based on the perceived future economic prospects of that country including the issuing country's expected growth in gross domestic product (GDP), inflation, level of debt and other factors. The reason gold or silver has historically increased in value is not because of the change in gold or silver, but rather the relative devaluation of the currencies of all the countries of the earth

HOW TO CALCULATE GROSS WEIGHT

You can calculate the gross weight if you know fineness and gold weight. The equation is 31.1035 multiplied by net weight in troy ounces divided by the fineness. An example: 31.1035 multiplied by .2354 divided by .9667 (result is 7.574 grams).

throughout the ages.

There is a cost to manufacture, distribute and market a gold bar or coin, and this cost is added to the precious metal value in the bar or coin and referred to as the premium. The premium also includes the profit of the distribution channel to move the bar or coin from the refiner or sovereign mint to the retail buyer.

The premiums vary on each brand (or issuer) of the bar and for each sovereign mint. In addition, the premium varies as a percentage of the value of the precious metal content, for small content such as 1/10 ounce to more content such as 1 ounce or more in a single bar or coin. The fact is that the manufacturing cost is about the same to make a 1/10 ounce gold coin as it is to make a 1 ounce gold coin. As a result, the fixed manufacturing cost as a percentage of the gold value in a 1/10 ounce gold coin is much higher than the same manufacturing cost as a percentage of the gold value of a 1 ounce gold coin.

Consider these examples:

EQUIVALENT	MARKET PRICE	RETAIL PRICE	PREMIUM
1 oz Gold	$1,496.40		
Gold Maple Leaf	$1,549.32	$1,556.26	3.56%
U.S. Eagle	$1,567.10	$1,578.70	4.75%
1/4 oz Eagle	$411.40	$418.98	10.00%
1/10 oz Eagle	$172.04	$179.57	15.00%
Silver Eagle	$39.27	$41.22	9.65%

This table (using gold at $1,496 an ounce and silver at $35.82 an ounce) shows that an intended bullion coin such as the Maple Leaf or the uncirculated American Eagle, has disparate premiums or the price that is paid by each for specified quantities of gold. When you buy a gold 1/10 oz. Eagle, the premium is about 15 percent (the equivalent of spending about $1,720 for an ounce of gold).

If you want to contrast, consider these examples. Gold on May 7, 2011, was $1,496.60. A Canadian Maple Leaf with 1 ounce of gold had a small premium (just under 4 percent), but it cost about $53 over the bullion or "spot" price. The U.S. Eagle with 1 ounce of gold was $18 more (a 4.75 percent premium)

This quarter eagle was minted under authority of the Act of Jan. 18, 1837, and weighed 4.17 grams. Its metal content then was $2.50. Today, its gold content is over $175. The coin's actual size is 18mm.

than its comparable bullion price. But to buy a 1/4 ounce U.S. Eagle was like buying gold at $1,645 an ounce (about a 10 percent premium), and for those buying in 1/10-ounce increments, the premium was about 10 percent and the cost-per-ounce was about $1,720.

Silver, whose price per ounce remains historically lower than gold's, has a premium of about 9 percent for a single 1 ounce Eagle coin. So how do you determine if a coin is considered numismatic (collectible) or bullion?

If a gold or silver coin sells at the market spot price of the metal, plus about 15 percent or less for the premium, it's probably a bullion coin. If its price is far above the spot price of the metal, it's a numismatic coin that is valued for more than the mere weight of its metal by collectors.

Almost all coins struck for circulation started out as pure bullion issues, with their metal content equal to their face value. Over time, some had the good fortune to acquire numismatic or collectible value as well. So the Washington quarter or the Bust half dollar or even the Morgan dollar have two components: the metallic composition and the numismatic worth. Depending on the surrounding marketplace, that may make it bullion one day and numismatic the next.

The ancients used alluvial gold, mined gold and mixtures of gold and silver (electrum) for part of their commerce. Coins evolved as a means of standardizing the weight and avoiding the need to assay the precious metal to assure its composition, metallic content and value.

"IN 1933, THE U.S.
SNEEZED, THE WORLD
ECONOMY CAUGHT
PNEUMONIA, AND
GOLD WAS VIRTUALLY
OUTLAWED EXCEPT FOR
COLLECTORS OF 'RARE
AND UNUSUAL COIN.'"

CHAPTER 3

How Some Metals Became 'Precious'

Gold and silver were known to the ancients. Platinum was unknown prior to the 16th century and was not available in large quantities until around 1750, when the Spanish found it plentiful in Peru. Palladium was not discovered until the time of Napoleon at the start of the 19th century.

Each of these precious metals has been the subject of long-standing political drama. Silver and gold have made headlines in the U.S. Some people wanted to corner the silver market, some wanted to take gold out of the hands of the American public. Platinum and palladium, white silver-like metals, have been the subject of international dispute and intrigue, largely because of their industrial use in catalytic converters.

Some of many bullion coins in the marketplace today.

METAL	1970	1980	1990	2000	2010	4/22/11
Gold	$37	$595	$378	$274	$1,405	$1,505
Silver	$2	$16	$4	$5	$31	$46
Platinum	$121	$580	$414	$619	$1,755	$1,825
Palladium	$34	$300	$80	$920	$760	$749

The highest compounded rate of return goes to gold hands down from 1970 to 2011, but in the short run, despite the big numbers, silver is the outstanding precious metal, doing one-fifth better than gold during the same time frame as the chart and graph show below:

10-YEAR COMPOUNDED RATE OF RETURN 2002-2011	
Gold	17.13%
Platinum	12.97%
Palladium	8.28%
Silver	25.97%

But in the long run (1970-April 22, 2011), gold overpowers all of them, with silver a close second:

41-YEAR COMPOUNDED RATE OF RETURN 1970-2011	
Gold	9.54%
Platinum	6.26%
Palladium	7.70%
Silver	8.48%
Dow	6.82%

In the past three or four years, we've seen extraordinary price swings in the precious metals market. But it hasn't always been that way. Gold has logged centuries of price stability. From 1792 when the U.S. Mint was founded until the present, the official price of gold has changed only four times. In 1834, the dollar was devalued from $19.39 an ounce to $20.67. That rate then held nearly a century, until FDR devalued the dollar by 59 percent to $35 an ounce.

In its own turn, gold was officially changed again in 1971 to $38 an ounce, and finally in 1973, President Nixon re-set the dollar, devaluing it to $42.22 an ounce of gold, the present rate, even though the market price is over $1,400 an ounce.

Gold has reached back and recaptured popular imagination as it first reached heights not seen in more than 30 years – $800 an ounce – but then jumped higher. In the last third of the Ought Decade (August 2008) gold had been over $800 an ounce on more than 160 days of the year. The price in March 2011 was over $1,400 an ounce, and in April, over $1,500. While platinum is higher, a 40-year price history shows ups and downs.

A look at the average annual price for gold, silver, platinum and palladium is revealing, especially when looked at over the last half century from 1960 until the present. They show the unnatural rise of 1979-80, a dramatic retreat, then a steady, progressive, solid increase that has brought it to present levels and suggests a push beyond. This is true for gold, and the same has held true of silver ($35 an ounce as gold topped $1,400, a 40:1 price ratio), platinum ($1,772 an ounce during the same time frame) and palladium ($755 an ounce in March 2011, while in late April 2011 with silver at over $48 an ounce, palladium retrenched slightly but gold jumped to over $1,527 an ounce, a 31:1 ratio).

AVERAGE ANNUAL PRICE PER TROY OUNCE OF METAL (A 50-YEAR HISTORY)

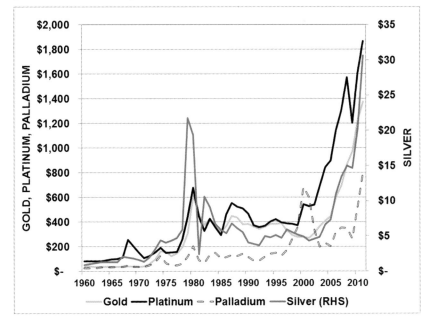

AVERAGE ANNUAL PRICE PER TROY OUNCE OF METAL (A 50-YEAR HISTORY)				
	GOLD	PLATINUM	PALLADIUM	SILVER
1960	$35.27	$83.21	$25.00	$0.91
1961	$39.25	$83.50	$25.00	$1.03
1962	$35.23	$83.50	$25.00	$1.20
1963	$35.09	$80.93	$31.00	$1.29
1964	$35.10	$88.48	$33.00	$1.29
1965	$35.12	$98.04	$34.00	$1.29
1966	$35.13	$99.60	$38.00	$1.29
1967	$34.95	$110.25	$38.00	$2.06
1968	$38.68	$256.33	$46.31	$1.96
1969	$41.09	$201.75	$38.19	$1.81
1970	$35.94	$151.67	$35.78	$1.64
1971	$40.90	$109.50	$35.04	$1.39
1972	$58.16	$124.38	$47.74	$1.98
1973	$97.32	$154.30	$75.45	$3.14
1974	$159.26	$192.37	$126.26	$4.39
1975	$161.02	$150.26	$66.28	$4.09
1976	$124.84	$153.29	$47.21	$4.35
1977	$147.71	$157.71	$49.34	$4.71
1978	$193.22	$260.81	$63.00	$5.93
1979	$306.68	$445.69	$119.83	$21.79

AVERAGE ANNUAL PRICE PER TROY OUNCE OF METAL (A 50-YEAR HISTORY)				
	GOLD	PLATINUM	PALLADIUM	SILVER
1980	$612.56	$677.31	$200.78	$19.39
1981	$460.03	$445.99	$90.58	$2.43
1982	$375.67	$327.42	$66.83	$10.59
1983	$424.35	$423.54	$136.16	$9.12
1984	$360.48	$356.73	$148.18	$6.69
1985	$317.26	$291.47	$105.76	$5.89
1986	$367.66	$461.59	$115.96	$5.36
1987	$446.46	$552.57	$129.95	$6.79
1988	$436.94	$525.29	$123.28	$6.11
1989	$381.44	$507.27	$143.70	$5.54
1990	$383.51	$466.95	$113.95	$4.07
1991	$362.11	$371.06	$86.93	$3.91
1992	$343.82	$355.81	$87.12	$3.71
1993	$359.77	$369.84	$120.30	$4.97
1994	$384.00	$401.46	$141.62	$4.77
1995	$384.17	$420.77	$149.94	$5.15
1996	$387.77	$394.88	$127.35	$4.73
1997	$330.98	$388.42	$172.40	$5.95
1998	$294.24	$384.73	$262.78	$5.54
1999	$278.88	$371.93	$358.02	$5.22

AVERAGE ANNUAL PRICE PER TROY OUNCE OF METAL (A 50-YEAR HISTORY)				
	GOLD	PLATINUM	PALLADIUM	SILVER
2000	$279.11	$544.03	$680.79	$4.95
2001	$271.04	$529.04	$603.82	$4.32
2002	$309.73	$539.13	$337.57	$4.59
2003	$363.38	$691.31	$200.27	$4.87
2004	$409.72	$845.31	$229.37	$6.67
2005	$444.74	$896.87	$201.37	$7.31
2006	$603.46	$1,142.31	$320.27	$11.04
2007	$695.39	$1,303.05	$354.86	$13.38
2008	$871.96	$1,573.53	$351.51	$14.98
2009	$972.35	$1,203.49	$263.27	$14.67
2010	$1,224.53	$1,608.09	$525.51	$20.19
2011	$1,375.65	$1,868.41	$805.39	$30.61
Apr. 28, 2011	1,535.50	$1,835	$777	$48.70
50 year avg	$330.83	$467.79	$168.37	$6.37
Median	$324.12	$378.33	$120.07	$4.82

For a long time, gold was a stable metal. Its price was fixed in the Mint Act of April 2, 1792, measured against silver, at about 15:1. In the years between, it has been at various ratios, showing that the marketplace and demand for each precious metal has changed over time. Today, gold is more than 40 times the value of silver.

Historic anomalies notwithstanding, gold's price stability was its attraction. As silver declined in direct proportion to the withdrawal of the

Comstock Lode and other mining scores from the ground, gold stayed stable in value until the Great Depression. Even then, it took devaluation of the dollar – really the re-valuation of gold to $35 an ounce – to regain stability.

That rate remained from 1934 until 1968, when the free market again took over. The price of the metal fluctuated, but within a narrow range. On Jan. 16, 1970, the price actually went below the official value (to $34.95 an ounce) before starting the inevitable upward progression.

Precious metal coinage reached its zenith during the last five years of the 19th century, probably because the Gold Standard Act of 1900 put the United States squarely in gold's corner, where it remained until 1933 when gold was effectively nationalized.

Following passage of the Coinage Act of 1873, millions of silver and gold coins were produced by the U.S. Mint and other world mints. The most common of those coins are bullion coins at today's high price of precious metal.

Contrasting gold's value with other currencies such as the euro, the yen and the British pound, shows that overall, the value of the metal stays in a narrow range among nations, even as the price of the metal has risen considerably over the last six years.

Just before the turn of the 20th century, it was obvious that it was a gold oriented world, but it was also a precious metal era. The old U.S. Mint reports focused on how much gold and silver was being mined, how much of the previously coined money was being submitted for re-coinage, and how much gold and silver was being shipped abroad, as well as imported, in settlement of obligations. Today when a nation needs to exchange gold, it is moved from one vault of the New York Federal Reserve in lower Manhattan to another. Back in the 1890s, it was shipped by sea, back and forth over the ocean.

America as a precious metal paradise was three generations away when the Great Depression of 1929 closed down the gold era. In 1933, the U.S. sneezed, the world economy caught pneumonia, and gold was virtually outlawed except for collectors of "rare and unusual coin."

Private gold ownership was restored on Dec. 31, 1974, and by the mid-1980s, American gold and silver Eagles led the world bullion parade. Platinum came next in 1997 and in 2010, the U.S. Congress authorized a palladium counterpart for issuance in 2011.

Putting the American experience of bullion into context, the marketing all started with South Africa's Krugerrand, followed by a number of look-alikes and substitutes in a variety of different precious metals. It's hard to say just when it reached the zenith, but the mintage figures of gold, silver and platinum Eagles don't lie: it's a precious metal paradise for those who want to acquire gold, silver, platinum or palladium.

Here's a listing of major modern precious metal bullion issues with first year of issue noted. Many have fractional issues, and nearly all have collector-based proof pieces that are also components.

GOLD	FIRST ISSUE	WEIGHT
United States (Eagle)	1986	1/10, 1/4, 1/2 and 1 oz
Canada (Maple Leaf)	1979	1/20, 1/10, 1/4, 1/2 and 1 oz
Australia (Kangaroo)	1986	1/10, 1/4, 1/2, 1, 2 and 10 oz and 1 kg
Austria (100 Corona)	1892	.9802 tr. oz
Austria (Philharmonic)	1989	1/10, 1/4, 1/2 and 1 oz
China (Panda)	1982	1/20, 1/10, 1/4, 1/2 and 1 oz
South Africa (Krugerrand)	1967	1/10, 1/4, 1/2 and 1 oz
Mexico (Centenario)	1921	1.2057 oz
Isle of Man (Angel)	1983	1/20, 1/10, 1/4, 1/2, 1, 5 and 10 oz
Mexico (Onza)	1981	1/20, 1/10, 1/4, 1/2 and 1 oz

SILVER	FIRST ISSUE	WEIGHT
Mexico (Libertad)	1982	1/20, 1/10, 1/4, 1/2, 1, 2 and 5 oz and 1 kg
United States (Eagle)	1986	1 oz
Canada (Maple Leaf)	1988	1/2 oz and 1 oz
Australia (Kookaburra)	1990	1, 2 and 10 oz and 1 kg
China (Panda)	1983	1 oz
Australia (Kangaroo)	1993	1 oz
United States (America the Beautiful)	2011	5 oz
United Kingdom (Britannia)	1997	1/10, 1/4, 1/2 and 1 oz
PLATINUM	FIRST ISSUE	WEIGHT
United States (Eagle)	1997	1/10, 1/4, 1/2 and 1 oz
Canada (Maple Leaf)	1988	1/20, 1/10, 1/4, 1/2 and 1 oz
Australia (Koala)	1988	1/4 oz
China (Panda)	1987	1/20, 1/10, 1/4, 1/2 and 1 oz
Isle of Man (Noble)	1983	1/20, 1/10, 1/4, 1/2 and 1 oz

MEASURING PRECIOUS METALS

Precious metals in coinage are measured in grains.
The conversion amount is 1 grain = 0.00208333333
troy ounces

"Nearly 100 years after John Maynard Keynes declared gold 'dead' as a currency ... the metal still stands strong."

CHAPTER 4

Gold Shines Through History

Gold has been precious since ancient times. It was revered amongst the Aztecs and in ancient Egypt where it is recorded in hieroglyphs, the source probably being the mines of Nubia. Gold is evidenced in the Balkans at the Varna Necropolis, which was decorated with gold 4,000 years before the birth of Jesus .

One of the earliest stories of the power of gold came about in the 8th century B.C. when Midas was supposed to have the golden touch – all that he came into contact with turned to gold. The myth took a semblance of reality with King Croesus, the last King of Lydia (died circa 547 B.C.), who was one of the ancient world's richest men. His fabulous wealth included the first gold coinage (made of electrum, a crude composition of gold and silver), and for more than 1,500 years his name was synonymous with gold and riches.

Since the time of Croesus, gold has had a preeminent role in money, coinage and economics. Nearly 100 years after John Maynard Keynes declared gold "dead" as a currency and almost 80 years after President Franklin Roosevelt confiscated domestic gold that wasn't in a coin collection, the metal still stands strong.

Though gold fluctuates in the daily marketplace, it has served as an asset of last resort and as an element that gives stability to the national economy of

Theodore Roosevelt's admiration of the fine arts resulted in the Mint commissioning famous sculptor Augustus Saint-Gaudens to design the $20 gold piece in 1907. Library of Congress photo.

a country, as well as granting it an international presence.

Just how to value gold has proven to be problematic. Sir Isaac Newton, the scientist who recognized that the falling apple on Tower Hill in London was governed by gravity, was more than a brilliant mathematician. He was also deputy master of the Royal Mint, the person in charge of coinage for the kingdom, and one of many who tried to first recognize and, then regulate, the apparent value and ratio of gold to silver.

In a famous tract written Sept. 21, 1717, at the Mint Office at Tower Hill, Sir Isaac wrote about how he sought to calculate value, a request the House of Lords asked of him.

Sir Isaac concluded that " By the course of trade & exchange between nation & nation in all Europe, fine Gold is to fine silver as 14 4/5 or 15 to one."

The 15 to 1 ratio established by Sir Isaac survived hundreds of years.

America achieved gold price stability in 1837, with the metal priced at $20.67 an ounce for nearly a century. FDR's devaluation of the dollar – raising the price at which the government would exchange gold to an ounce – kept the metal price stable for another 35 years.

The discovery of gold at Sutter's Mill by John Marshall in 1848 reshaped American history as well as its coinage. By the Act of March 3, 1849, Congress changed the unit of value from a silver dollar to a gold dollar coin and added a larger coin – the double eagle or $20 gold piece – to help sop up the gold coming from California. Soon, it was evident that there was so much gold being brought from the ground – the finds were richer and richer – that a mint was needed to supervise and standardize the production specification. And, by July 3, 1852, a branch mint was authorized in California together with an assay facility.

As usual, it took a while for other denominations to catch up. Not until 1853 did Congress finally get around to making a weight change in the half dollar, quarter, dime and half dime. They were made legal tender to $5, and the Mint was authorized to make bullion purchases.

Silver was a subordinated metal that didn't know it yet. Gold coins were being made at the

1889 Morgan dollar

Above, FDR nationalized gold. Photo courtesy Franklin D. Roosevelt Presidential Library. At left, a copy of the poster advising people of the proclamation recalling gold.

San Francisco Mint and shipped by sea to New York in a pre-Panama Canal era. It was still safer than a transcontinental rail route, since the railroad would not be completed until 1869. Meanwhile, silver and gold alike could be deposited at any mint of the United States and for .5 percent, refined and made into coin. Gold's price stabilized at $20.67 an ounce and silver jumped in value at the start of the silver war, but then held steady at $1.29 an ounce.

War creates its own crises, and in the American Civil War, there was a shortage of small change, a shortage of gold and silver, and a shortage of money in Treasury vaults with which to pursue the war. Neither metal remained stable, and soon there was competition in the form of paper money.

On April 28, 1870, Sen. John A. Sherman of Ohio proposed an amendment to the draft that called for an end to free coinage and the institution of a small fee for striking gold and silver coins from deposited bullion. But the amendment was ultimately defeated. In 1870, it was simply not profitable to turn silver bullion into coin. The Comstock Lode production had yet to flood the market, Indian Wars prevented massive extraction of silver bullion and its shipment east, and the price of bullion remained at such a level that it cost more than a dollar's worth of silver to make one silver dollar.

In 1870, when the Treasury made its proposal, the price of silver averaged $1.32 per ounce. It remained at similar levels throughout 1871 and 1872. When gold was discovered in California at Sutter's Mill in 1848, the forthcoming Gold Rush dug out more gold than the world had ever conceived possible to mine.

From a production of just 48,762 ounces in 1845, production rose in to 1,935,000 ounces in 1849. Each year thereafter until 1854, production increased. But even after 1854, more than $55 million in gold was being extracted annually, a far sight from the mere pittance of $889,085 extracted in 1847.

Gold began to flood the market, and the price of silver, as the only alternative money to gold, began to rise. Silver production was still in its infancy, for in 1859, just 77,300 ounces were mined, and this relative scarcity contributed to its monetary strength. But still, because it took more than a dollar's worth of silver to make a silver dollar under government specifications, few were coined by the U.S. Mint.

The discovery of the Comstock Lode in Nevada in 1859 and its exploitation a decade later was perhaps the single factor that ultimately undermined the strength of silver. It was apparent to many people, including Dr. Henry Linderman of the Mint, that silver could be potentially produced in far greater quantities than the previously inconceivable gold extraction. As time was to prove, he was right, and from 1867 until the coinage legislation was actually law, the mint official set out to demonetize silver before a market oversupply would cheapen the price.

Just for the record, gold and silver are today the same gold and silver that has been used in commerce for more than 2,000 years. Gold is often called a currency without a country and the fact that today's currencies fluctuate in value relative to, for example, one ounce of gold or silver demonstrates not the movement of gold, but rather the change in the value of the currency of the issuing country. Currencies of countries change relative to one another and relative to gold and silver based on the perceived future economic prospects of that country including the issuing country's expected growth in gross domestic product (GDP), inflation, level of debt and other factors. The reason gold or silver has historically increased in value is not because of the change in gold or silver, but rather the relative devaluation of the currencies of all the countries of the earth throughout the ages.

Fabled 1933 $20. All of the known specimens came out of the Philadelphia Mint and through the hands of dealer Israel Switt. One example sold by Sothebys in 2002 for $7.59 million.

GOLD RESERVES FROM 1845 TO 1900 IN METRIC TONS

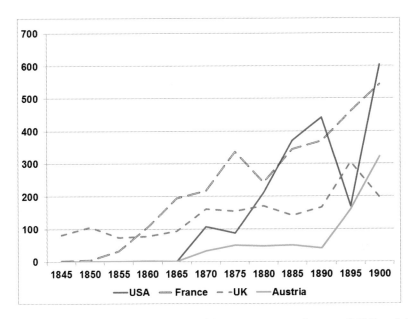

Note that the gold reserves of the United States were insignificant until 1865 and the world powers of the age were the United Kingdom and France. Source: World Gold Council.

As the nation moved toward the gold standard, it found little need for small-denomination gold coinage, and the Act of Sept. 26, 1890, discontinued the $3 and $1 gold coins. The Act of Nov. 1, 1893, may speak of bimetallism but by 1897, even as Congress planned for an international monetary conference, gold was moving toward a key role. The gold standard was made law of the land in 1900, though the politics of cheap (silver) money versus gold went on for another generation.

From the Roaring Twenties to the Great Depression, the economic life of the United States changed. By April 11, 1930, the quarter eagle or $2.50 gold piece was discontinued by an Act of Congress. The Depression deepened, economic hope appeared lost. Soon gold ownership was banned.

Only "rare and unusual" gold coins were exempt – enough to allow coin collectors to maintain and keep a collection, assuming that they would be able to do that during the depths of the economic despair of 1934.

Franklin Delano Roosevelt, governor of New York, was elected President in 1932. The drive to end the ownership of gold and the striking of gold coins began on March 6, 1933, just two days after FDR had braved the bitter snow in Washington to deliver his first inaugural address.

Roosevelt declared a "Bank Holiday" by invoking an obscure section of the 1917 Trading With the Enemy Act. The Act permitted the President to prohibit "under such rules and regulations as he may prescribe ... any transactions in...export or earmarkings of gold or silver coin or bullion ... by any person within the United States."

FDR closed the nation's banks by declaring that "there have been heavy and unwarranted withdrawals of gold and currency from our banking institutions for the purpose of hoarding; and ... these conditions have created a national emergency." During the banking holiday, Roosevelt prohibited the operation of any banking institution, prohibited any bank from paying out, exporting or earmarking gold or gold coins, and temporarily suspended the striking of gold coin by the Mint.

Roosevelt's action, one leading constitutional scholar, Henry Mark Holzer, wrote in a 1973 retrospective law review article, was probably illegal at best, and unconstitutional at its worst. Yet, the American people were desperate: a Depression gripped the land. Roosevelt, they believed, offered salvation – a New Deal, even if it was without gold. Some claim it made the 1933 $20 coin illegal to hold.

Systematically, Roosevelt acted to remove gold from the citizenry, the banks and the Federal Reserve. The key purpose of the action was to prevent any citizen from buttressing his currency against the debasement about to be perpetrated by the government.

The government's gold stock in 1933 consisted of $2.3 billion in bullion and $806.4 million in gold coin of various denominations. The Federal Reserve held $743 million in gold coin, and a fraction of that amount ($66.5 million) in bullion.

National banks had $141,000 in gold coin, while the public, state and private banks (other than national banks) had $310 million.

FDR next called a special session of Congress to deal with the crisis at hand. Set to commence on March 9, 1933, the session of the 73rd Congress would last less than 100 days. Yet, in that short period of time, Roosevelt accomplished more than any other chief executive in history.

Congress was bombarded with bills designed to put America back on her feet. The Civilian Conservation Corps (CCC) was enacted; the Agricultural Adjustment Act (AAA) was passed; the National Industrial Recovery Act (NIRA) was rammed through; the Thomas Amendment to the AAA gave the President authority to change the content and value of the dollar; the Tennessee Valley Authority Act (TVA) was quickly passed; a Federal Deposit Insurance Corp. (FDIC) was created; and the gold standard and gold clause were nullified.

Nullification of the gold clause, which had allowed citizens to demand payment in gold coin, was significant. Ironically, the use of the clause has renewed itself in the last decade of the 20th century by those seeking to preserve a standard of value measured against a fixed asset.

On March 9, 1933, the very day that the special session of Congress convened, Roosevelt submitted "The Emergency Banking Act" to them for consideration. He also sent them a message, stating that "On March 3 banking operations in the United States ceased....Our first task is to reopen sound banks."

The bill proposed that if the Treasury head, or really the President, determined that it was no longer in the national interest to allow private ownership of gold coin or bullion, individual Americans would have to give up their "hedge" against this.

Congress approved the procedure in an unusually fast way. The bill passed the House by voice vote at 4:30 p.m., barely four hours after it had been introduced. Promptly introduced in the Senate, that body ratified it at 7:30 p.m. An hour later, President Roosevelt signed the bill into law.

Further American action guaranteed convertibility of the dollar at the rate of $35 for each troy ounce of gold; American dollars abroad, offered by foreigners, were the lure since U.S. citizens universally lost the right to own most gold after Jan. 30, 1934.

"...ONLY 'RARE AND UNUSUAL' GOLD COINS WERE EXEMPT FROM FDR'S SEIZURE, ENOUGH TO ALLOW COIN COLLECTORS TO MAINTAIN AND KEEP A COLLECTION, ASSUMING THAT THEY WOULD BE ABLE TO DO THAT DURING THE DEPTHS OF THE ECONOMIC DESPAIR OF 1934."

CHAPTER 5

The Great U.S. Gold Melt

Gold coins turned in to the government in 1934 were melted by the U.S. Mint, cast into bricks or bars and eventually shipped to Fort Knox. The stake: for the previous century, 351 million gold coins worth $4.5 billion had been struck in the form of 174 million double eagles, 57 million eagles or $10 gold pieces, 78 million half eagle or $5 gold pieces and 20 million quarter eagles or $2.50 gold pieces. There were also 539,000 $3 gold pieces and 19.8 million $1 gold coins produced.

Prior to the start of the great coin melts of 1933-1935, $145.7 million in U.S. gold coins had already been melted. Of the $4.5 billion in gold coins that had been produced from the U.S. Mint's first year until 1933, something on the order of $3.1 billion worth of U.S. gold coinage had also been exported.

Of the surviving coins that were not melted, only "rare and unusual" gold coins were exempt from FDR's seizure, enough to allow coin collectors to maintain and keep a collection, assuming that they would be able to do that during the depths of the economic despair of 1934.

In 1954, a ruling was made that any gold coin made prior to 1933 would be considered to be a rare gold coin. Any gold coins made after 1933 would be presumed not to be rare unless a specific determination to the contrary was made by the Treasury.

President John F. Kennedy, August 1962, in the Oval Office, shortly after an executive order issued prohibiting Americans from owning gold abroad except under license.

Prior to 1961, the holding of gold in any form outside of the United States was not controlled by the Treasury Department. However, on Jan. 14, 1961, Executive Order 10905 prohibited the holding of gold abroad by any person subject to the jurisdiction of the United States. An exception was made for gold coin of recognized special value to collectors or rare and unusual coin.

A number of countries began issuing restrikes of coins made prior to 1933 and there has also been an appreciable amount of counterfeiting of gold coins abroad. As long as these coins remained outside of the United States, it was difficult for the Treasury Department to determine whether the coins being held were actually those ruled to be exempt.

On July 20, 1962, Executive Order 11307 was issued, which provided that except under a license, no persons subject to the jurisdiction of the United States may acquire, hold in their possession or have any legal or equitable interest in any gold coins situated outside the United States unless it is determined to be of exceptional numismatic value.

The criteria determining the exceptional numismatic value of an issue of gold coins are based upon the number issued, the purpose of the issue and all other factors concerning the issue. Not all pre-1933 gold coins are now admissible, including certain United States gold coins. The criteria are of necessity very strict.

Persons subject to the jurisdiction of the United States have been prohibited from holding mutilated gold coins within the United States since 1933 and outside the United States since 1961. Any solder on the coin or the drilling of a hole in it constitutes mutilation.

The importation of restrikes into and the holding of restrikes within the United States have never been permitted. In addition, restrikes may not be held abroad by persons subject to the jurisdiction of the United States. Restrikes are subject to forfeiture in the hands of purchasers, no matter how innocent.

In 1968, President Lyndon set up a two-tiered market for gold based on the official price of $35 an ounce, and a free market price that was permitted to float somewhat higher. The price of gold jumped, moving to heights of $43 an ounce, which caused a sensational ripple in the coin market, because double eagles traditionally traded at a price about 48 percent above the spot price of gold. Overnight, they went from $48 to $60 for uncirculated coins.

In summary, gold coins were traded and available on a widespread basis, even British sovereigns of the modern era – but if any were made after 1960, they could not be legally imported into the United States without a permit from the Office of Domestic Gold and Silver Operations.

Leland Howard, director of the Office of Domestic Gold and Silver Operations.

Dr. Leland Howard, an assistant director of the U.S. Mint, became head of the ODGSO, and his task was to protect the integrity of the Roosevelt seizure order, while simultaneously allowing rare and unusual coin to be imported.

Eventually, an arbitrary line in the sand was drawn with 1960 as the demarcation point. Before that, it was rare and unusual, even if it was a 1958 sovereign with 8.7 million pieces produced. Afterwards, it was common and not importable with a license, even if it was a 1962 sovereign with 3 million pieces manufactured.

The humor of this governmental regulation of the economy can be seen with thousands of words of government regulation that then resulted to try and explain what was rare and unusual; why and how some items were prohibited, while others could be imported.

As gold faced the real market for the first time following 1968, it was inevitable that economic forces that traditionally had driven the price upward – inflation, war and economic fears – could, in the converse, drive its price down.

And so it did in the early days of 1970. By Jan. 16, 1970, Under Secretary of the Treasury Paul Volcker (later Chairman of the Federal Reserve) announced that the new gold agreement signed with South Africa provided "no assured 'floor price' for gold speculators," and with that, the metal

Thomas Wolfe, Director of the Office of Domestic Gold and Silver Operations, with the author, Washington, D.C., 1968.

dropped to its lowest price in London free trading in 16 years: below the official floor of $35 an ounce.

The events of January 1970 were liberating. In a totally free market, gold could rise or fall – and without an official price or a floor, as Volcker put it, the metal price could go below an official buy price of the government.

Ironically, within 18 months, inflation would be ravaging the nation, and on Aug. 15, 1971, President Nixon would suspend the dollar's convertibility into gold, slamming down the gold exchange window and setting the stage for the dramatic rise of gold – and the numismatic market – for decades to come.

Once again the dollar was devalued, raising the official price of gold to $38 an ounce. But ironically, with or without an official price, the run on the metal

GOLD BUGS

Government officials constantly warned that private gold ownership was only one step away from economic disaster. They took their pronouncements seriously, and indeed, rumors could cause gold's price to spike 50 cents or a dollar. That sounds minuscule, but in those days, if the Dow Jones average rose or fell 10 points, it made the first page of the newspapers, not just a small particle in the financial section.

Starting in the early 1970s, a group of "gold bugs" began to advocate private gold ownership rights and eventually, they found the ear of some congressmen and senators who bought into their fairness theory and the claimed illegality of the gold seizures and recalls of the 1930s.

In a truly bizarre episode, they tacked a resolution allowing for private gold ownership onto the foreign aid package that the Nixon Administration wanted. Presidential vetoes were threatened and an alarmist attitude prevailed at the Main Treasury building.

The foreign aid bill with its non-germane gold ownership clause finally made it to a vote in which conservative members such as Rep. Phil Crane, R-Ill., and others voted with liberal Democrats. Crane said to me later it was the only foreign aid bill that he voted for in his 35-year congressional career.

His rationale: it was more important to get private gold ownership than argue the vagaries of a single year's foreign aid package.

proved the historic truism that gold was and still is king of precious metals.

Gold's high point in the half century after the New Deal, probably came in the inflation-ridden late 1970s and early 1980s when interest rates topped out at 21 percent for home mortgages, and the price of the metal rose to $800 an ounce. Its nomenclature as an asset of last resort was proven again and again as refugees from all parts of the world used modest quantities of the metal, strapped to their bodies, as they escaped to freedom and a new life financed by the shiny, yellowish metal.

On Dec. 3, 2001, U.S. Federal Reserve Chairman Alan Greenspan spoke to a group in New York in which he wistfully recalled the role that gold once had (0.05 ounces of gold and .77 ounces of silver had the same value, namely, 1 dollar) at the time of the Coinage Act of 1792.

At the same time, he strongly spoke in favor of the euro, the new European currency coming Jan. 1, 2002, noting that its backing was dependent on the overall economy, not any particular precious metal.

Greenspan's analysis, however, came from a position of strength. There were then, as now, some 261 million troy ounces of gold under management of the Treasury Department with a book value of $11.04 billion and a free-market value in 2001 of $71.8 billion. In 2011, just a decade later, this asset of last resort is still carried on the books at $11 billion, but is now worth about $365 billion on the free market.

Of possibly more interest is that the Federal Reserve Bank of New York has 73,451.741 troy ounces of unspecified gold coins in its vaults, which presumably are pre-1933 U.S. gold coins. This amounted to over $2 million melt value at the time of Greenspan's speech, and in 2011, the value stood at $105 million. If they once were $20 gold pieces, it amounts to about 76,000 pieces.

There are also about 2.9 million ounces valued $4.1 billion in "working stock" at Mint headquarters in Washington, D.C., in offsite warehouse space, at the Philadelphia Mint and at West Point. By far, the West Point Mint has the largest share with over 2.1 million ounces consisting of coins, blanks and miscellaneous. The "miscellaneous" material includes bars, unsold coins and condemned coins (those not made according to specification).

For much of gold's American history, its value was $20.67 an ounce. And at that level, from 1837 to 1933, the bulk of American gold coins were made.

A $20 gold piece contained $19.99 worth of gold, a $10 gold piece contained .48 troy ounces or just a bit less than $10 worth of gold, and proportionally downward.

The very stability of gold and its fixed value is what made it so attractive in times of distress and times of inflation. For that very reason, it was deemed an essential part of the New Deal economic recovery plan to remove from American citizens the ability to own gold.

This is an oversimplification, but the New Deal's aim was to inflate the economy. The way that it did that was to revalue gold from $20.67 to $35 an ounce. The $20 gold piece thusly contained about $33.86 worth of gold, an instant profit that FDR and his advisers did not want to give to the population as a whole.

Coin collectors, of course, were exempt by special presidential edict, but with limitations. No more than four of each date and type of rare and unusual coin were permitted to be owned.

Americans continue to have an attraction to gold perhaps because there is so little of it around. A frequent example cited by the South African Bureau of Mines is that if all the gold in the world mined from the time of the Lydians was melted and poured into a mold the size and shape of the Washington Monument, it would not even go halfway to the top.

Add to that an element of some economic uncertainty and it's not hard to figure out just why, for well over 2,000 years, gold has been an asset of choice, and why it remains so popular with collectors, who know that the numismatic value, the additional element of scarcity, only enhances its worth.

"FROM AUGUST 1978 UNTIL NOW, GOLD HAS GONE UP, DOWN, AND SIDEWAYS."

CHAPTER 6

U.S. Restores Private Gold Ownership

In 1973, gold regulations were eased slightly to allow more gold coins minted between 1933 and 1961 to be admitted to the country as "rare" coins. By early 1974, the President had gained the legal ability to allow private gold ownership whenever he felt the international economic situation made it in the best interest of the United States.

Gold ownership finally came about in one of the most unusual unifications of interest of diverse political elements: the conservative "gold bugs" and the liberal democrats.

Succinctly, the Democrats had a foreign aid package that was in need of passage. The conservative Republican "gold bugs," most of whom had voted against every foreign aid proposal, saw a truly golden opportunity.

They added a clause to the foreign aid bill that would simultaneously legalize private gold ownership by a certain day, but also retroactively repeal all of the regulations and laws that impeded holding the precious metal.

The unusual political coalition held together, the foreign aid bill became law, and on Dec. 31, 1974, private gold ownership was again permissible for the first time in 40 years. Gold's historic role once again moved to preeminence.

From August 1978 until now, gold has gone up, down, and sideways. But those who would have bought bullion then (or gold medallions when they were finally authorized in November 1978 by Public Law 95-620, and issued in 1980 and afterwards) didn't do that badly.

The return on investment from 1978 to 2011, 33 years, is about 6.2 percent annually, compounded. It outpaced inflation, which averaged 3.3 percent during the same period. The rare coin fund index that Salomon Brothers used to compare measurements shows rare coins advanced 8.5 percent during the same period.

Putting this all in some kind of perspective, the last 35 years of private gold ownership, or gold acquisition, has been a bit of a roller coaster ride. But with the ups and the downs, gold has remained an asset of historic importance, one that is likely to be looked at, collected and utilized for quite some time to come.

ALL GOLD IS NOT CREATED EQUAL

You can buy gold in a variety of forms:

GOLD STOCKS AND FUNDS – Buying stock in a gold mining firm or buying into a mutual fund that invests in gold bullion is a common way to invest in gold. Most brokerage firms buy and sell these financial instruments. Gold stocks and mutual funds may offer more liquidity than actual gold, and there's no need for an investor to store or protect gold investments purchased in this form.

BULLION AND BULLION COINS – Bullion is a bulk quantity of precious metal, usually gold or silver, assessed by weight and typically cast as ingots or bars. Many major banks and dealers sell bullion. Bullion coins are struck from precious metal, usually gold or silver, and kept as an investment. They are not used in daily commerce. The value of bullion coins is determined mostly by their gold or silver bullion content rather than by rarity and condition. The prices change daily, depending on the prices for gold and silver in the world markets. Major banks, coin dealers, brokerage firms and precious metal dealers sell bullion coins. The U.S. Mint has produced gold, silver and platinum bullion coins for investment purposes since 1986 and guarantees their precious metal content.

COLLECTIBLE COINS – These coins have some historic or aesthetic value to coin collectors. Most collectible coins have a market value that exceeds their face value or their precious metal content. This so-called collectible value is often called numismatic value. The coin dealers who sell collectible coins often have valuable coins graded by professional services, but grading can be subjective.

"JUST AS THE SPANISH,

SOUTH GERMAN AND

HUNGARIAN MINES WERE

DIMINISHING IN THEIR

SILVER PRODUCTION,

A NEW WORLD WAS

DISCOVERED BY THE

VOYAGES OF EXPLORATION."

CHAPTER 7

Silver: The Early Choice for Coins

Silver has been a symbol of wealth, value and money since ancient times. The earliest known of all coinage, that of Lydia (circa 750 B.C.), was made from electrum, an alloy of gold and silver.

Almost 800 years earlier, in the Bible's Book of Genesis (13:2), the wealth of the patriarch Abraham is described as being "very rich in cattle, in silver, and in gold."

Silver was traded by weight (known as shekels) starting around 3000 B.C., but the marking of the electrum coinage in what is modern day western Turkey is what truly began the rise of silver as both a method of payment and as an early investment.

Being far more plentiful than gold, silver was first mined in western Turkey, but the Greeks brought mining to a fine art form at Laurium, not far from present-day Athens. From about 600 B.C. to 300 B.C., the Laurium mines probably produced about a million ounces of silver a year, according to the Silver Institute, an industry trade organization.

Later, there were mines in Spain that, for nearly a millennium, produced enough silver to satisfy first the needs of the Roman Empire, then Carthage, and ultimately most of the world's needs, along with those of southern Germany and the Austro-Hungarian Empire.

1881-S silver dollar was originally struck as a bullion product.

Most estimates today say that from the Laurium era (600 B.C.) to the 1500 A.D., mining operations totaled about 1.5 million ounces of silver each year. About 31.5 million ounces were produced during this era.

Just as the Spanish, South German and Hungarian mines were diminishing in their silver production, a New World was discovered by the voyages of exploration. Given that one purpose of their journey was the discovery of more gold and silver sources, they succeeded beyond their wildest expectations.

Silver was the first metal discovered by the Conquistadores in New Spain, making good the investment of King Ferdinand and Queen Isabella in a fleet of vessels designed to take the riches of South and Central American silver mines and fill the coffers in Madrid.

By the mid-1530s, a Casa de Moneda, or mint, had been built in Mexico City, the first in the new world, and more followed in rapid progression throughout the growing Spanish empire. A determination was made that the new world was going to give up its bounty to the Royal Treasury of Castille– which the Spaniards did, striking Pieces of Eight coins to fill the hull of the wooden boats to transport the mother lode back to Spain.

Three centralized locations and good Spanish records, suggest that Mexico produced about 1.5 billion troy ounces of silver between 1500 and 1800 and that the Potosi region of Bolivia also produced around 1.5 billion troy ounces to complement Mexico. And Peru, from about 1600 to 1800, averaged 3 million ounces a year or 600 million ounces total, taking us to the cusp of the

19th century when the American discovery of the Comstock Lode created a disorderly displacement in the precious metals market.

Silver today is mined in 58 countries including Mexico, the U.S. and Canada. Gold, by contrast, is mined in 76 countries. All told, about 24 times more silver than gold has been mined.

Through the years, silver coins and silver bullion have been an important component of many collectors' and investors' portfolios. Some common-date silver coins have had more value as a bullion-like item than for numismatic worth. This was particularly true in 1980 when the Hunt Brothers' attempt to corner the silver market brought the price of silver up to nearly $50 an ounce, at which time 1964 Washington quarters (mintage 704 million pieces from the Denver Mint) suddenly found that their metal content gave them a worth of more than $8 a coin. Up until that point, that particular coin was little more than a spacer with no material value. Now the bullion content alone gave substantial worth for even the most common of silver coins. More significantly, it became a bullion investment and collectible.

Stocks go up in value too, but coins are not like stocks. They have a fixed supply, and the government manufacturer stops minting the current version at the end of the year and moves on to the next one. Fixed supply creates scarcity if there is sufficient demand, and it is this scarcity that drives the coin industry.

When the United States was founded as a nation, the writers of the Constitution were leery of the colonial experience with currency "Not worth a Continental" and banned issuance of "money" that was not gold and silver.

The 1964 quarter is worth over $8 when silver nears $50 an ounce as it did in 1980.

SILVER ANNUAL AVERAGE PRICE PER OUNCE 1928-2011

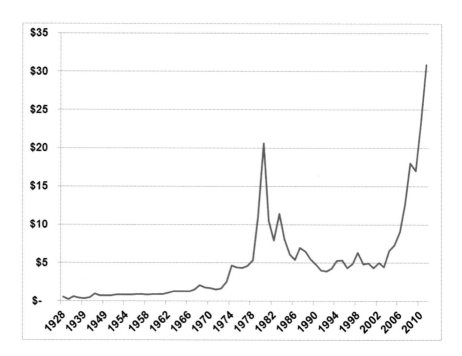

That didn't mean copper coinage couldn't be issued for change, and indeed, just three years after the Constitution was adopted, the Mint Act of 1792 called for gold, silver and copper coinage.

The original Mint Act of 1792 was Alexander Hamilton's broad vision complemented by Jefferson's views of how a currency system should be managed. During the country's first 100 years, little was changed in the U.S. coinage system. It wasn't until the Coinage Act of 1965 was passed that the country saw fundamental alteration in minting and coinage law.

Even before the Constitution was signed, the Founding Fathers showed concern about how to legislate the composition of money. Hamilton suggested that a gold to silver ratio of 15:1 be utilized for valuation purposes. Hamilton may have been correct in his economic analysis, but by the time that the legislation was enacted, the ratio of world price had slipped to about 15.5:1, and as a result, silver was too inexpensive. Coins that were produced promptly left circulation. Until the early 1830s, the imbalance was not corrected – accounting for modest availability of gold coinage from that era.

Neil Carothers, whose book, *Fractional Money*, remains a classic more than 80 years after it was published, calls the original coinage system (1792-1828) "a discreditable failure." The Spanish pillar dollar remained the principal unit of value, and as Carothers succinctly put it, "Spanish coin could not be driven out until the mint provided domestic coins in abundance." Actually, the pillar dollar remained legal tender until Congress changed the law and eliminated the ability to use the coin in 1857.

The Coinage Act of 1837 attempted to re-balance the appropriate ratio, and priced gold at $20.67 an ounce (or equivalent) and made silver worth $1.29 an ounce. Gold remained at the fixed number for nearly a century (it would be re-valued in 1933 by President Roosevelt). Silver was less lucky.

Citizens under the earliest elements of this system had the right to deposit silver or gold bullion with the mint and receive, in return, a full measure of precious metal coinage, less the cost of coining. The government and the population could thus control currency supplies. The right to deposit these metals was called "free coinage," though this was hardly so since there was a modest charge by the Mint for the service.

Millions of ounces of silver were purchased and turned into coin, but as all of the warnings in the 1860s suggested, as the market flooded with silver, the price of the metal continued to go down. As the years progressed, the Mint bought silver, turned it into coin, received the coin back, re-coined it, and the process seemed circular. In fact, this melting and organized re-coining of non-current coin makes silver dollar mintage figures meaningless. The same is true for subsidiary coinage.

A Jefferson nickel

Subsidiary coinage (half dollar, quarter, 20-cent piece, dime and 3-cent silver coin) was produced to meet the needs of small change. Silver dollars made a political statement.

Silver dollar production, suspended in 1873 for circulating coins, resumed in 1878 with the passage of the Bland-Allison Act over the veto of President Rutherford B. Hayes. But while that aspect of the Coinage Act of 1873 was set aside, the rest remained.

Resumption legislation caused silver to be bought by the Treasury and coins to be minted. When silver was needed, the coining stock was culled; during World War I, the Pittman Act resulted in the destruction of millions of silver dollars.

The "New Deal" offered by President Franklin Delano Roosevelt offered price support for those in the business of mining and producing silver. They needed it. From a high price in 1874 of $1.29, silver went into a decline that reached 65 cents an ounce in 1900 and a low of 24.5 cents an ounce in 1933. The 1933 Annual Report of the Director of the Mint says the Mint purchased 1.3 million ounces of silver at an average cost of 27 cents an ounce and even in the midst of a Great Depression, silver used in the arts was estimated at 24.2 million ounces.

Even as this was happening, acting under the Executive Proclamation of Dec. 21, 1933, the Mint and Assay offices of the United States were authorized to receive in the four succeeding years domestically mined silver at a price equal to the monetary value (64.6 cents) which compared to an open market price of 43 cents, according to the 1934 Annual Report of the Director of the Mint.

Then, a further boost to the miners over and above the price subsidy came. A silver purchase act was approved on June 19, 1934, which directed an increase in the silver monetary stack. The aim: raise it to a quarter of the gold monetary stock.

The 1934 Mint Report characterizes what can next be described as a significant change: "This act also directed issue of silver certificates against silver bullion, authorized the coinage of standard silver dollars, and authorized nationalization of silver, which was proclaimed by the President August 9, 1934."

An Office of Domestic Gold & Silver Operations was established in the Treasury Department. Its licensing authority was terminated by Executive Order 11825 on Dec. 31, 1974, and the office was finally disbanded July 31, 1975.

Enter World War II and there was a real need for silver again, this time as a substitute for nickel, an important war material. "War nickels" were authorized by Congress on March 27, 1942, to take the place of the copper-nickel 5-cent coin because copper and nickel were both critical war materials used for munitions.

The actual act by Congress called for 50 percent silver and 50 percent copper, but gave authority for other changes if public interest warranted. To distinguish the coins further, and to allow for their later withdrawal from circulation, large mintmarks labeled "P," "D" and "S" were placed above the Monticello dome on the reverse.

The weight of the coin's pure silver consisted of 0.05626 troy ounces, which at 40 cents an ounce made the coins worth about 2.2 cents for their metal content. By 1961, when the Treasury stabilized the price of silver bullion at $1.29 an ounce, it made War nickels worth 7 cents apiece. At the height of the silver boom in 1980, when the price of the metal topped $48 an ounce, they had about $2.70 worth of metal in each coin. At around $35 an ounce today, the nickels are worth about $2.

Approximately 870 million War nickels were produced from 1942 to 1945 using about 50 million ounces of silver from the strategic reserve. That same reserve was utilized until just recently to produce American Eagle bullion coins.

When the war ended, nickel was restored, and silver moved to the rear guard.

And so it was until the early 1960s. Silver was mere backwater.

Gradually the price of silver increased, an event that would not only affect the coin industry, but also the American economy. It began innocently enough in 1961 when the price of silver went from 91 cents an ounce to $1.04. By the following year, it had risen to a high of $1.22, and in 1963, the price hit $1.29, the level at which melting silver coins became theoretically possible.

As of 1963, the Treasury Department still honored the contractual verbiage contained in silver certificates, and redeemed each certificate for a single silver dollar. Hoards of silver certificates were redeemed on this pledge causing a virtual run on the Treasury. In the process, bags of rare silver dollars, many dated 1903 from the New Orleans Mint, were discovered. Pieces of eight – Spanish silver coins about the size of a silver dollar – which had previously been scarce, plummeted in price virtually overnight from $1,500 per coin to $30 a coin.

Now, nearly a half century later, it still has not fully recovered its old value.

Still, as these coins gained in value, they became worthwhile candidates for melting. Conveniently, the Mint recorded in its various annual reports what denominations were melted. Like gold, this happened starting in the 1890s. The following data has been assembled going through Mint records, showing destruction of significant numbers of silver coins. Here's a summary:

AMERICAN SILVER COINS MINTED AND MELTED (STATISTICS)					
DENOMINATION	MINTED	MELTED	NET AVAIL	% MELTED	% AVAILABLE
Dollars	855,661,153	325,437,470	530,223,683	38.03%	61.97%
Trade dollars	35,965,924	1,721,332	34,244,592	4.79%	95.21%
Half dollars	1,790,917,250	171,608,886	1,619,308,364	9.58%	90.42%
Quarters	4,449,108,957	282,924,148	4,166,184,809	6.36%	93.64%
20¢	1,355,000	411,298	943,702	30.35%	69.65%
Dimes	10,055,455,835	337,500,473	9,717,955,362	3.36%	96.64%
Half Dimes	97,605,388	1,348,669	96,256,719	1.38%	98.62%
3¢	42,736,240	21,805,398	20,930,842	51.02%	48.98%
TOTAL	17,328,805,747	1,142,757,674	16,186,048,073	6.59%	93.41%

These coin melts make the case for an unexpected numismatic bonus for those who want to acquire bags of silver coins – the 90 percent silver coins struck in 1964 and earlier – and which are widely traded among coin dealers and some who invest in bullion that is in coin form (it is of course also available in bars format). Legal tender coins, even in bulk, remain a preferred method for collectors.

The Coinage Act of 1965 fundamentally changed American coinage since it removed silver from the circulating dime and quarter, reduced the silver composition of the half dollar (and removed at year's end in 1970) and authorized various prohibitions against the melting of coins as determined by the Secretary of the Treasury.

The event also ultimately brought the government into the coin business as a full-fledged partner, since in the course of cleaning house and dealing with silver, a hoard of 2.9 million rare Carson City minted silver dollars was found in the Treasury vaults.

That hoard, eventually sold by the General Services Administration for tens of millions of dollars, was the government's first experience with selling coins as an investment. It made a lasting impression and formed a basis for commemorative coin sales programs and marketing efforts of the Mint in later years that proved durable and successful, raised hundreds of millions of dollars in funds, and assisted in popularizing coin collecting and coin investing with the American public.

Gold bullion coins were introduced in September 1986, and by year's end its silver counterpart, the silver Eagle, was minted. Complete sell-outs of proof versions of both of these popular 1986-dated pieces occurred. By 1991, tens of millions of the silver coins had been issued. A generation later, the quantities seem astronomical, for by 2011, more than 250 million ounces of silver have been sold by the U.S. Mint, most of it directly to consumers.

The United States Mint has produced special commemorative coins intended for collectors since 1892. That year a silver commemorative half dollar coin was issued in honor of the 400th anniversary of Columbus's discovery of the New World. From 1892 until 1954, the U.S. Mint produced 144 different commemorative coins in silver in three denominations: one 25-cent coin, a silver dollar, and the rest 50-cent pieces. There were also nearly a dozen gold coins of various sizes and denominations.

Commemorative coins abused the purpose of coinage, but served a salutary purpose: commemoration and raising of funds for various groups and endeavors. That proved its undoing, and by 1930, President Herbert Hoover vetoed a commemorative coin bill passed by Congress. That set the stage for vetoes by all succeeding presidents through Dwight D. Eisenhower, though

Silver was the metal of choice for U.S. coins until the late 1900s.

some measures made their way through.

The commemorative coinage system of the 1930s and 1940s became so abused that it was shut down in 1954. It was ultimately resumed in 1981 to commemorate the bisesquicentennial of the birth of George Washington. Other issues followed, each approved by Congress and all manufactured and sold by the United States Mint. By 1987, U.S. Mint sales to collectors and investors topped the $1 billion mark, the equivalent of a Fortune 500 company.

It's useful to know that a coin always maintains its status as a medium of exchange, whether its value rises or falls below a par value. For example, in 1919, the selling price of silver rose above the nominal value of American currency when the price of silver topped $1.38 an ounce. A silver dollar, struck in 1904 or earlier contained .7734 troy ounces of silver. Silver in the coin was valued at $1.06, more than face value

Given all of this, how much silver coin was produced? Of that, how many did the U.S. Mint itself melt through the years?

The U.S. Mint has contributed significantly to distribution of silver into the marketplace. Since its silver 1 ounce Eagle bullion coin was first issued in 1986, more than 203 million troy ounces of silver have been sold, mostly to investors making purchases of several ounces at a time. (There is also a total of several million proof ounces that can be added to gross sales.) In the last two years alone, more than 45 million ounces of silver have been sold as 1 ounce Eagles.

One of the reasons that silver has had such intense activity over the last several years, after a hiatus in the early 1980s, is that industrial demand has outstripped supply in virtually every year since 1990. Mine production hovers at between 300 to 400 million ounces per year. Nearly all silver production is done ancillary to other mining, that is, as a by-product of mining some other metal that incidentally yields silver.

"BUT, PROSPECTIVE

PURCHASERS MAY

ASK, HOW CAN THE

MARKET BE HOT

WHILE NEW COIN

SALES ACT SO SLOW?"

CHAPTER 8

Platinum and Palladium Join the Club

Platinum is a metal on the move. In June 2003, the price was $600 an ounce. At the end 2011, it was back over $1,500 an ounce. Not a bad amount for investors.

Translating this to coin sales for the U.S. Mint platinum program has been tough sledding, however. Of 10,000 platinum proof sets (consisting of a 1 ounce, 1/2 ounce, 1/4 ounce and 1/10 ounce), just 3,178 of 10,000 available 2004 sets had been sold as of mid-November at the issue price of $2,495 – probably a case of sticker shock.

But 1 ounce uncirculated issues aren't moving appreciably better. In November 2004, just 2,200 coins (representing 1,600 troy ounces of precious metal) were produced by the Mint for distribution by its special dealer network.

But, prospective purchasers may ask, how can the market be hot while new coin sales act so slow? The answer is a telling one that reveals one of the great secrets of the platinum market: its drawing power abroad, especially in China, whose affinity for the metal and huge potential demand fuels the fire.

Platinum bullion coins are not the exclusive province of the U.S. Mint. Australia, Canada, China and South Africa are key players in the bullion

PLATINUM AVERAGE ANNUAL PRICE

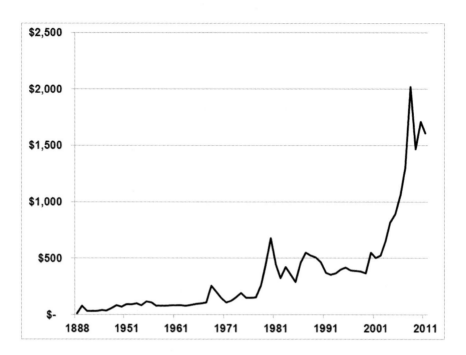

market, with other countries marketing bullion products and non-circulating legal tender issues.

To put the platinum bullion coins in a historic context, gold and silver have been mined since antiquity, and gold and silver coins have been produced for over 2,000 years. By contrast, platinum has a history that is only 450 years old.

Discovered by Italian scientist Julius Scaliger in 1557, large quantities of platinum were not available until about 1750, after the Spaniards found platinum in Peru.

They named it platinum from the Spanish word "plata," which means silver, a way of describing the actual grayish color of the metal. Miners frequently refer to it as white gold because it can be found in beds of gold-bearing sand.

Early numismatic use of the metal swiftly followed. A platinum medal was produced commemorating the discovery of the metal in large alluvial quantities. Platinum coinage began in 1763 from dies normally utilized for the Columbian 8-escudo gold coin, and would continue to be struck through 1819.

Chile, Bolivia and Peru also made unsuccessful attempts at issuing platinum coinage, as did Spain, which produced at least 13 varieties of patterns between 1776 and 1904 in the silver-grey colored platinum metal, and a number of regular issues.

Even into the 1960s, there were new discoveries of platinum coinage issues. In 1962, dealer Jerry Cohen discovered a platinum 1867 10-escudo piece (before then, the only known specimens were dated either 1866 or 1868).

Like gold, platinum can be found in nugget form. In 1843, a 21-pound lump was found in Russia, which regularly issued platinum coinage for circulation from 1828-1845 in the 3-, 6- and 12-ruble.

Mintages for the 3-ruble coins of the 1830s show how well-accepted the coin was in Russia. More than 106,000 pieces were produced in 1830 and some 86,500 the following year. In 1832, some 65,767 pieces were produced. By 1842, a total of 145,578 pieces were coined.

One of the heaviest substances known, about 21 times the weight of water of the same volume, platinum is easy to shape like gold and silver and does not tarnish. Chemically described as the 78th element on the periodic table, it has a high density of 21.5 grams per cubic centimeter and a substantial melting point of 1,772 degrees Celsius (3,224 degrees Fahrenheit).

Most platinum is not mined by those seeking it as a singular metal; rather, it is a byproduct of mining for other metals, mostly non-precious with industrial use. It is the most valuable impurity of most nickel deposits.

Other platinum group metals such as ruthenium, palladium, osmium and iridium are similarly found and mined. All of this combines to make platinum among the rarest of metals and the scarcest of coins.

About 60 years after platinum's major commercial availability began, the U.S. Mint produced its first platinum pattern coin, a half dollar dated 1814 described by Dr. J. Hewitt Judd in his book, *United States Pattern, Experimental & Trial Pieces,* as an experimental piece from regular dies.

This wasn't the last American experience with platinum coinage before the modern era. By the early 1840s, researcher Nick Parker wrote, "the stepped up production of platinum made it worth even less than silver," the result of which was counterfeit gold coins made of platinum.

Russia's experience with platinum began in 1814 when Czar Alexander I struck the first commemorative medal in platinum, commemorating the capture of Paris. The metal was imported, but by 1824, platinum was being produced in the Ural Mountains of Western Siberia.

Since then, a review of literature and auction catalogs reveals a number of platinum coins available to the collector. One major source for information is the collection of Edwards H. Metcalf, a California collector who developed a penchant for platinum coinage in the 1940s. When his collection was sold by Superior Galleries in Beverly Hills in October 1987, it was probably the largest single auction of platinum coinage .

Among the Metcalf coins not otherwise generally known as platinum pieces is a 25 dinars of Andorra dated 1960 (type of Krause-Mishler 1), and comparable for 1963, 1964 and 1965. Yet despite the rarity – just two pieces in platinum are known – the prices were very reasonable: from $484 to $577.50 in the prices realized.

Other countries' platinum coinage represented included: Bhutan (1966 set, one of 72 produced), Bolivia (8 escudos from 1782, Potosi mint), Columbia (8 escudos of 1801), Denmark, France, Germany-Prussia, Britain, Haiti, Hawaii, India, Iran, Isle of Man, Italy, Japan, Lesotho, Liechtenstein, Macao, Madagascar, Mexico, Monaco, Panama, Poland, Russia, Spain (4 and 8 escudos), Switzerland, Tonga and Venezuela.

But the American bullion coin program, though steeped in the history of platinum as a metal, really has its origins in the successful bullion program that has been run by a number of other countries over the past decade. Among them: Canada, China, Mexico, Australia, Isle of Man and Russia.

Unlike gold, whose basic uses are jewelry, coinage and a storehouse of value, platinum's rarity is derived at least in part from its industrial and technological uses, though Chinese jewelry is no longer insignificant.

Here are some of the basic statistics on platinum, palladium and the platinum-group metals.

Yearly, more than 1 million ounces are involved in industrial use,

2009 Platinum Eagle

1.84 million ounces in jewelry consumption, and 3 million ounces for auto catalyst demand. Other industrial users include chemical, electrical, glass and petroleum industries.

Platinum in investment products – coins and bars – is estimated at about 235,000 ounces, according to Johnson Matthey's precious metal marketing division. Johnson Matthey is a refiner, marketer and fabricator of precious metals in some 25 countries.

Prices of platinum have reflected the steady demand, rising from between $340 to $350 an ounce in 1991 to more than $1,500 an ounce in 2011. For the most part, platinum trades at a small premium above the price of spot gold.

Platinum is mined principally as an off-product of other metal acquisition; a significant amount comes from nickel. Canadian ore principally comes from International Nickel Company (Inco), which recently pulled 2,650 tons a day from the mine to yield 200,000 ounces of platinum and 410,000 ounces of palladium.

The mathematics of this is mind-boggling. This means that 967,250 tons (1.9 billion pounds) of ore (rock and metal) had to be moved in order to recover 16,666 pounds of platinum and about double that amount of palladium.

The U.S. Geological Survey offers a different perspective on all this. Last year, they wrote in their annual report, "The price of platinum averaged $762 per ounce in November, the highest level since February 1980. Higher prices were not totally the result of a shortage of the metal. As with gold and many other metals, funds have been buying platinum. Their interest is for technical reasons as well as concerns about production delays."

PLATINUM AND PALLADIUM: PRODUCTION, IMPORTS, EXPORTS (REPORTED IN OUNCES)

	2006	2007	2008	2009	2010e
MINE PRODUCTION					
Platinum	4,290	3,860	3,580	3,830	3,500
Palladium	14,400	12,800	11,900	12,700	11,600
IMPORTS FOR CONSUMPTION:					
Platinum	114,000	181,000	150,000	183,000	153,000
Palladium	119,000	113,000	120,000	69,700	71,000
Rhodium	15,900	16,600	12,600	11,200	13,000
Ruthenium	36,000	48,700	49,800	21,200	14,000
Iridium	2,800	3,410	2,550	1,520	3,500

PLATINUM AND PALLADIUM: PRODUCTION, IMPORTS, EXPORTS (REPORTED IN OUNCES)

	2006	2007	2008	2009	2010e
Osmium	56	23	11	68	14

EXPORTS:

	2006	2007	2008	2009	2010e
Platinum	45,500	28,900	15,600	15,600	19,000
Palladium	53,100	41,800	26,400	30,300	35,000
Rhodium	1,600	2,210	1,980	1,220	2,200
Other PGMs	3,390	8,190	6,450	4,020	5,400

PRICE DOLLARS PER TROY OUNCE:

	2006	2007	2008	2009	2010e
Platinum	$1,144	$1,308	$1,578	$1,208	$1,600
Palladium	$323	$357	$355	$266	$500
Rhodium	$4,561	$6,203	$6,534	$1,591	$2,500
Ruthenium	$193	$574	$325	$97	$198
Iridium	$349	$444	$448	$420	$635

U.S. production of platinum and palladium is presently limited to two facilities, the Stillwater mine at Nye and the East Boulder mines in the Beartooth Mountains of Montana. Both mines are owned by the same company. A total of 373,000 tons of ore were mined, yielding 63,000 ounces of platinum and 207,000 ounces of palladium in 1994. Recently, North American produced about 225,000 ounces of platinum against a regional demand of about 1 million ounces.

The collecting community is likely to be enthusiastic for the proof bullion coin, a true first that is likely to be viewed in much the same way that proof gold and silver Eagles were in 1986.

About 1.44 million proof silver Eagles were sold in 1986 against 5.9 million uncirculated bullion ounces, and 446,290 ounces of gold proof 1 ounce ($50 face) coinage was utilized against 1.362 million ounces of uncirculated bullion gold coinage.

Platinum historically has sold less than gold, but much less metal is available. In 1995, when the Johnson Matthey estimate of platinum coin demand was 75,000 ounces of coins, gold coins produced from the top 10 issuers of pure gold coinage (Austria, Iran, Australia, U.S., Canada, Isle of Man, South Africa, P.R. China, Turkey, Mexico and all other countries) aggregated 3.3 million troy ounces of coins.

Platinum is the potential winner of the decade of the Oughts (2010-2019). It has the demand, it lacks sufficient production quantity and is the investor's darling. There seems to be a future for platinum bullion and non-circulated legal tender coins.

The U.S. Mint will introduce a $25 face value palladium bullion coin with a Mercury-head design and a weight of 1 ounce in 2012.

Palladium, a member of the platinum group of precious metals, has had a volatile history over the last three decades as it looks for its place in the precious metals wanderlust. Its high point came in 2001 when it briefly rose above $1,000 an ounce. Its average price since 2006 is about $360 an ounce. Currently, its trading range is above $750.

Today, only Canada mints palladium bullion coins. The attraction of an American palladium bullion coin to Congress and the marketplace is the price point relative to gold and platinum. Even as gold and platinum have jumped to new heights, the price of palladium ranged substantially lower; the average price in 2007 was $355 per troy ounce. In fall 2011, it traded at $569 an ounce.

Time will tell whether palladium proves to be attractive to collectors and investors.

"THEY EACH EXPLOITED

A LOOPHOLE THAT

PERMITTED COIN

COLLECTORS TO

KEEP UP TO FIVE

SPECIMENS OF EACH

DATE AND MINTMARK

WITHOUT BEING IN

VIOLATION...."

CHAPTER 9

History of Buying U.S. Gold Bullion Coins

In 1961 it was illegal for most Americans to own gold. That didn't stop entrepreneurs like Louis Eliasberg of Baltimore or New York attorney Harold Bareford from holding gold. It also didn't stop John Jay Pittman, a chemical engineer from Rochester, N.Y., who worked for Eastman Kodak Company. They each exploited a loophole that permitted coin collectors – actually those who acquired "rare and unusual coins" – to keep up to five specimens of each date and mintmark without being in violation of the Executive Orders that otherwise recalled gold coinage to the melting cauldrons of the 1930s.

Bareford collected gold coins mostly from the early 1940s until 1954. Pittman collected from the 1930s to the 1990s and Eliasberg from the 1930s until 1976. Pittman was probably the most experienced collector with the best eye. Next was Bareford, and finally Eliasberg, who acquired whole collections to obtain coins that he needed.

Harold Bareford circa 1943. Photo courtesy William Bareford.

Between 1941 and 1954, Bareford bought gold bullion in the form of

John Jay Pittman (L) then president of the American Numismatic Association, with Rep. Wright Patman, D-TX, chairman of the House Banking Committee, Rep. Leonor K. Sullivan, D-Mo., chairman of the Consumer Affairs subcommittee, and the author, circa 1973, after Pittman told the committee America deserved a circulating bicentennial coin in 1976. His suggestion was the quarter, which Congress later adopted.

coins. Some were true rarities, but most coins were not worth much over their dollar value in gold. FDR devalued the dollar by about 59 percent, raising the price of gold from $20.67 an ounce to $35. In the process, a $20 gold piece suddenly had $33.86 worth of gold in it. Many of Bareford's coins were modestly priced over their gold cost. An 1836 $5 gold piece (in brilliant uncirculated condition) was bought by Bareford for a little more than double face value – $10.20.

Bareford's gold coin collection was sold by Stack's in a 242-lot offering that had originally cost the lawyer $13,832.15. The 1978 resale price was an incredible $1.2 million. Many of the coins have since sold for a lot more.

Every coin in the catalog experienced substantial growth, some as much as 100 times what Bareford paid for it more than three decades earlier. Most of the coins were in uncirculated condition or were choice proofs, and the 275 people in attendance made for active bidding.

It's worthwhile remembering that Harold Bareford purchased gold coins

PITTMAN BULLION COINS ($5 Gold all sold Oct 21-23, 1997. Gold Weight 0.241875.)						
LOT	Date & description	Purchase Price	Purchase date	Price per troy ounce	Selling price	Compounded net gain
995	1851 v. ch. unc	$150.00	1963	$620.16	$46,750	18.40%
997	1851-O F-VF x-Stacks Baldenhofer	$25.00	1955	$103.36	$468	7.22%
999	1852 unc x-Michael Higgy -Kosoff	$15.00	1943	$62.02	$6,600	11.93%
1000	1852-c vf Kosoff	$27.50	1957	$113.71	$1,540	10.59%
1002	1853 au Elser, Higgy(Kosoff)	$15.00	1949	$62.02	$1,045	9.24%
1006	1854-d xf BM DOUGLAS	$28.50	1957	$117.84	$4,400	13.43%
1007	1854-o vf New Netherlands 50th	$19.00	1957	$78.56	$1,430	11.41%
1008	1855-c vf KRIESBERG SCHULMAN	$51.00	1959	$210.87	$1,210	8.69%
1020	1858-D vf x-Stacks Baldenhofer	$25.00	1959	$103.37	$1,210	10.75%
1093	1908 Ch. AU Lib. head x-George Bauer	$10.50	1946	$43.42	$467.50	7.73%

John Jay Pittman (1913-1996) had an eye for coins and collected them seriously. He bought coins at coin shows, coin club meetings, at auction and from the stock of well known dealers. In this chart, which shows some exemplars of $5 gold pieces, JJP is shown as paying anywhere between $43.42 and $117 an ounce (two non-bullion pieces show a counter-example). David W. Akers auctioned the collection, and the unit cost of JJP's profit is also shown. Two other coins are shown as a point of contrast.

in his collection under the "rare and unusual coin" exemption that the Treasury Department created. Still, Bareford bought many coins that were not stellar rarities, but rather everyday gold coin where the dominant element of its worth – and the reason for its acquisition – was the modest premium over the cost of the gold itself. Some of these coins were acquired for more than bullion or bullion-like price.

PRECIOUS METAL

Measurement is in grains, grams, and troy ounces.
- 1 grain (1 gr) = 0.064799 g (Grams)
- 1/7000 pound; equals a troy grain or 64.799 milligrams
- 31.103 5 grams = 1 Troy ounce
- 12 troy ounces = 1 troy pound
- 1/2 grain 0.032399 grams
- 1/4 grains 0.016199 grams
- 516 grains = 33.4362 grams

The 1869 $3 gold coin that Bareford bought from a Hans M.F. Schulman sale in 1951 for a mere $28 has an interesting history. The price paid for the coin is the equivalent of about $193 an ounce for the gold, which is a bit more than semi-numismatic, but not extraordinary given the prices of the era. The buyer of the 1978 Bareford sale was Harry Bass, a serious collector, later president of the American Numismatic Society and creator of the Harry Bass Foundation in whose name the collection was cataloged (you can still see it online) and ultimately sold. Offered as lot 484, it was long removed from the bullion and semi-numismatic component that it once was labeled, and the grade assigned by Schulman rated the coin as MS-65, or Mint State 65, a condition exactly as the coin left the U.S. Mint. The price realized: $29,900.

Louis Eliasberg's gold coin collection is not materially different except that it was virtually complete by the time that it was sold as the "U.S. Gold Coin Collection" in 1982. My notes say that when the family turned the collection over for auction by Bowers & Merena in the early '80s, he was one coin down: an 1866 "no motto" $20 gold piece from the San Francisco Mint.

Five years after Eliasberg, Bowers & Merena was holding "The King of Siam" sale in New York on Oct. 14, 1987. In that catalog, lot 2043 for an 1866-S "no motto" $20 gold piece in EF-40 or Extremely Fine, a nice but circulated coin, is described as "finer" than the Eliasberg coin. There is a paragraph added in small type:

"When the cataloger studied the Eliasberg Collection prior to presenting it

1908-D double eagle $20 gold coin

at auction in 1982," Bowers wrote, "it was discovered that the collection had no 1866 "no motto" double eagle [$20 gold coin]. Whether Louis Eliasberg overlooked the variety or whether he considered his collection complete because he had an 1866-S "with motto" is not known. However, in the interest of completeness the Eliasberg family purchased one through us, and we acquired it from dealer Neil Berman." So as a footnote to numismatic history, the Eliasberg Collection was "completed" in 1982 with Neil Berman furnishing the missing piece!

Pittman's acquisitions were the best chronicled at the time. Many were displayed at the Rochester Coin Club, some were bought at public auction, and each told a story. Pittman's collection was sold in 1997-1999 in a series of sales by David W. Akers for over $40 million. But again, the story at the time was the price jumps from low-cost rarities that became six-figure items. For purposes of this book, it's more interesting to note the bullion or bullion-like prices paid by Pittman at acquisition compared with their still phenomenal results.

The chart on page 100 shows some gold half eagles ($5 gold pieces) from

LOT	Date & Description	Purchase Price	Purchase date	Price per troy ounce	Selling price	Compounded net gain
	PITTMAN BULLION COINS (U.S. $20 Gold pieces. Gold Weight 0.9675.)					
1118	1850 AU Elser, Higgy(Kosoff)	$60.00	1949	$62.02	$1,980.00	7.56%
1120	1850-O VF Stack's 10/30/1964 lot 969	$97.50	1964	$100.78	$2,750.00	10.65%
1122	1851-O AU Ed Bell	$125.00	1963	$129.20	$8,800.00	13.33%
1123	1852 unc Elser, Higgy(Kosoff)	$60.00	1949	$62.02	$5,500.00	9.87%
1124	1852-O Ch. AU C. Foster	$75.00	1952	$77.52	$4,125.00	9.31%
1125	1853 Ch. AU Elser, Higgy(Kosoff)	$60.00	1949	$62.02	$7,150.00	10.47%
1127	1854 Unc Elser, Higgy(Kosoff)	$60.00	1949	$62.02	$10,450.00	11.35%
1130	1855 XF x-Frank T Manship	$48.00	1961	$49.61	$429.00	6.27%
1132	1855-S Ch Unc x-B Max Mehl (Jerome Kern)	$87.50	1950	$90.44	$9,350.00	10.45%
1133	1856 Unc Elser, Higgy(Kosoff)	$60.00	1949	$62.02	$11,825.00	11.64%
1137	1858 Unc Elser, Higgy(Kosoff)	$60.00	1949	$62.02	$14,300.00	12.08%
1144	1866-S VF x-Toivo Johnson	$46.00	1956	$47.55	$1,320.00	8.53%
1184	1906-D Ch Unc Tampa Show	$50.00	1962	$51.68	$407.00	6.17%
1191	1908-D Ch AU Stacks	$42.00	1956	$43.41	$4,950.00	12.34%
1204	1912 Unc Stack's	$60.00	1959	$62.02	$1,650.00	9.11%
1208	1913-S AU Dallas Coin CO	$55.00	1955	$56.85	$1,760.00	8.60%
1227	1926 Ch Unc x-William Donner	$55.00	1955	$56.85	$715.00	6.30%

John Jay Pittman bought a number of double eagles at the equivalent of face value or slightly more. He had an eye for quality, even with bullion and semi-bullion purchases.

the Pittman collection, all of the 1850s, each (except the first) purchased on bullion or near bullion conditions. Note that the rate of return on each (compounded) is substantial for the bullion, bullion-like and non-bullion coin (which is offered just as a point of contrast).

It is easy to be dismissive by calling this a proposition that works with lower denomination gold coins, but John Jay Pittman shows that this was common practice with double eagle ($20) gold coins too. Consider this table of more than a dozen coins, some in well-circulated condition, the others in about uncirculated or even better, and see how a knowledgeable collector (and investor) was able to buy gold coins in the 1950s and '60s at what was essentially a bullion price. The bulk of these double eagles cost between $43 and $77 an ounce. Some were auction purchases, others were private purchases.

This 1851 $20 gold coin graded Mint State-61 was acquired by John Jay Pittman around 1949 from Ralph Elser for $60 (rough equivalent of gold at $62 an ounce). When David W. Akers auctioned his collection, it brought $3,080. At the January 2002 FUN show, it was a $4,370 coin. Akers and others also give the coin a pedigree to the Higgy collection. Numismatic Gallery (1943, Kosoff) sold the Michael F. Higgy Collection at public auction, but examination of the catalog's dozen gold coins shows an 1850 double eagle, but not the 1851.

"Some of these coins are struck with 'accidental' but intentional numismatic value – modern issues from a number of countries – whose primary purpose is to sell the precious metal…"

CHAPTER 10

Bullion Coins Hit the American Market

The sale of gold bullion coins to private collectors began modestly more than 50 years and grew into a multi-billion dollar industry. At the start, the force came from outside the United States where the Bank of Nova Scotia began selling gold coins into the U.S. market.

In the early 1960s, the Bank of Nova Scotia began to offer so-called "bullion" coins or semi-bullion coins into the U.S. market, the first organized attempt to sell wholesale quantities of foreign gold coins to American collectors and investors. They issued irregular price lists and charged a modest premium, and since these coins were for the most part "rare and unusual," they were permitted entry.

The first list in January 1961 included just the U.S. quarter eagle ($2.50), half eagle ($5), eagle ($10) and double eagle ($20) gold pieces, along with the British sovereign and half sovereign, and the Swiss 20-vreneli. The list also included 25-, 50- and 100- gram wafers, however these items could not be imported into the States.

On July 5, 1961, Bank of Nova Scotia added the Dominican Republic's 30-peso, the 20-franc "Napoleon" of France, the 10-franc piece and the heavy 1.2 ounce Mexican 50 pesos. Almost a year later, price list 32 (March 28, 1962) distinguished between old sovereigns and new sovereigns and carried the footnoted caveat that coins minted after 1933 could not be legally imported into the US. This also applied to 1 and 4 ducats, Austrian restrikes dated 1915.

Some of the coins on the list didn't qualify. That had a lot to do with the Office of Domestic Gold and Silver Operations ("ODGSO"), which was created to manage the aftermath of the gold recall of 1933-1934. They maintained a list of coins that met the "rare and unusual" exception and those that did not.

Eventually, a bright line was drawn by ODGSO separating pre-1959 coinage (legal to own as "rare and unusual") and the 1960 issues (not so rare or unusual).

Today, there are different types of bullion coins: (1) the "pure" bullion with weights of 1/20, 1/10, 1/4, 1/2 and 1 or more ounces, produced by several sovereign governments in uncirculated condition, (2) a proof version also produced by sovereign governments and intended primarily for collectors, and (3) the gold coin originally intended for circulation which has primary value in bullion, but which has a slight numismatic premium (generally not more than 15 percent above the spot price on any given day). This includes:

- Mexican 50-peso pieces ("The Centenario") (1.2098 troy ounces of gold)
- U.S. Saint-Gaudens $20 gold pieces in circulated condition (.9675 tr. oz.)
- Old British sovereigns, minted and circulated prior to H.R.H. Queen Elizabeth II (.2354 tr. oz. of gold)
- French Rooster (20-franc), well circulated (.1867 tr. oz.)
- Swiss 20-franc (vreneli) (.1867 tr. oz.)

The Bank of Nova Scotia began selling foreign bullion coins like the French 20 francs, nicknamed "The Rooster," in the early 1960s.

- Russian Chevronetz (10 roubles) (.2489 tr. oz.)
- Colombina 5 pesos (.2354 tr. oz.)
- Italian 20 lire (.1867 tr. oz.)
- U.S.$2.50 Indian and Liberty head (.1209375 tr. oz.)
- U.S.$5 Indian and Liberty head (.241875 tr. oz.)
- U.S.$10 Liberty (.48375 tr.oz.)
- U.S.$20 Liberty or Saint (.9675 tr. oz.)

These recent bullion coins are issued almost entirely for their precious metal content. These are coins where the issuing authority is satisfied to make a 2 percent or 5 percent premium over the spot price of the metal to cover manufacturing and other costs. Occasionally, due to low mintages, they have an added enhancement: numismatic value. Some of

The 1780 Maria Theresa Thaler is a silver bullion coin.

these coins are struck with "accidental" but intentional numismatic value – modern issues from a number of countries – whose primary purpose is to sell the precious metal, whether it be gold, silver, platinum or palladium.

Many of these coins are of recent origin, although the date may be much older, due to several world mints engaged in the practice of issuing restrikes. It's true for gold and silver issues. For example, the Maria Theresa Thaler, bearing a 1780 date, is a circulating trade coin now in its third century of use.

But besides these trade coins, there is a significant production issue of 1 ounce and fractional precious metal coins from some of the following countries:

GOLD
- United States (Eagle)
- Canada (Maple Leaf)
- Australia (Nugget)
- Austria (100 Corona)
- Austria (Philharmonic)
- China (Panda)
- South Africa (Krugerrand)
- Mexico (Centenario)

A variety of gold bullion coins issued worldwide

SILVER
- Mexico (Libertad, "Liberty," or Onza, "ounce")
- United States (Eagle)
- Canada (Maple Leaf)
- Australia (Kookaburra)
- Austria (Maria Theresa Thaler, dated 1780 restrikes)

PLATINUM
- United States (platinum Eagle)
- Canada (platinum Maple Leaf)
- Australia (platinum Koala)

PALLADIUM
- A U.S. palladium coin was authorized by Congress in 2010 for issuance in 2011 and beyond.

Examples of bullion coins (clockwise from left): gold Mexican 50 Peso, silver Mexican Onza, Australian Kookaburra.

These coins often come in multiple denominations or fractional interests. Occasionally, there are coins larger than an ounce. In 2010, the U.S. Mint began production of 5-ounce silver coins as part of the America the Beautiful design.

Many people like to buy, sell and trade bullion coins, take their profit, and then reinvest in either another or different precious metal, a precious metal coin or another vehicle. A cautionary note to those inclined to take this route: the IRS takes the position that bullion coins and other bullion products are not similar in the least, and more importantly, that they are not "alike."

The meaning of this is clear. You can't exchange a bullion product of identical weight with a legal tender gold coin without there being a tax consequence. You may think it's the same, but your favorite Uncle has a competing view that has negative tax consequences for you (the exchanger).

In general (but not always), the uncirculated bullion and semi-bullion coins have a different cost per ounce (or cost-range) than proof pieces do. Most bullion acquirers want the lowest cost per ounce. The numismatic value gives it a different component – and value at the same time.

On the next chart appear the prices and premiums for various bullion coin products on March 18, 2011:

BULLION COIN OR BAR	COUNTRY OR REFINER	VALUE OF PRECIOUS METAL	PREMIUM	TOTAL	% PREMIUM
GOLD					
Eagle 1 oz.	United States	$1,417.50	$67.37	$1,484.87	4.75%
Eagle 1/2 oz.	United States	$708.75	$56.70	$765.45	8.00%
Eagle 1/4 oz.	United States	$354.38	$35.43	$389.81	10.00%
Eagle 1/10 oz.	United States	$141.75	$21.26	$163.01	15.00%
Buffalo 1 oz.	United States	$1,417.50	$75.79	$1,493.29	5.35%
Maple Leaf 1 oz.	Canada	$1,417.50	$46.32	$1,463.82	3.27%
Maple Leaf 1/2 oz.	Canada	$708.75	$56.70	$765.45	8.00%
Maple Leaf 1/4 oz.	Canada	$354.38	$42.53	$396.90	12.00%
Maple Leaf 1/10 oz.	Canada	$141.75	$22.68	$164.43	16.00%
Maple Leaf 1/20 oz.	Canada	$70.88	$12.76	$83.63	18.00%
2008 Olympic Maple Leaf 1 oz.	Canada	$1,417.50	$54.74	$1,472.24	3.86%

BULLION COIN OR BAR	COUNTRY OR REFINER	VALUE OF PRECIOUS METAL	PREMIUM	TOTAL	% PREMIUM
2009 Olympic Maple Leaf 1 oz.	Canada	$1,417.50	$84.22	$1,501.72	5.94%
2010 Olympic Maple Leaf 1 oz.	Canada	$1,417.50	$105.28	$1,522.78	7.43%
Maple Leaf .9999 1 oz.	Canada	$1,417.50	$60.25	$1,477.75	4.25%
Philharmonic 1 oz.	Austria	$1,417.50	$46.32	$1,463.82	3.27%
Krugerrand 1 oz.	South Africa	$1,417.50	$46.32	$1,463.82	3.27%
Panda 1 oz.	China	$1,417.50	$99.23	$1,516.73	7.00%
100 g bar	Pamp Suisse	$4,557.26	$148.90	$4,706.17	3.27%
10 oz. bar	Johnson Matthey	$14,175.00	$319.97	$14,494.97	2.26%
5 oz. bar	Pamp Suisse	$7,087.50	$202.10	$7,289.60	2.85%
SILVER					
Eagle 1 oz.	United States	$35.82	$3.45	$39.27	9.65%
90% Pre-1965,$100 Face	United States	$2,561.13	$52.86	$2,613.99	2.06%

BULLION COIN OR BAR	COUNTRY OR REFINER	VALUE OF PRECIOUS METAL	PREMIUM	TOTAL	% PREMIUM
90% Pre-1965, $1,000 Face	United States	$25,611.30	$413.09	$26,024.39	1.61%
Maple Leaf 1 oz.	Canada	$35.82	$3.34	$39.16	9.32%
Wolf 1 oz.	Canada	$35.82	$13.87	$49.69	38.71%
Grizzly Bear 1 oz.	Canada	$35.82	$11.54	$47.36	32.23%
2008 Olympic Maple Leaf 1 oz.	Canada	$35.82	$5.77	$41.59	16.10%
2009 Olympic Maple Leaf 1 oz.	Canada	$35.82	$6.93	$42.75	19.35%
2010 Olympic Maple Leaf 1 oz.	Canada	$35.82	$8.09	$43.91	22.58%
Koala 1 oz.	Australia	$35.82	$12.13	$47.95	33.87%
Koala 10 oz.	Australia	$358.20	$57.77	$415.97	16.13%
Koala 1 kilogram	Australia	$1,151.61	$103.99	$1,255.61	9.03%
Kookaburra 1 oz.	Australia	$35.82	$10.98	$46.80	30.65%
Kookaburra 10 oz.	Australia	$358.20	$46.22	$404.42	12.90%

BULLION COIN OR BAR	COUNTRY OR REFINER	VALUE OF PRECIOUS METAL	PREMIUM	TOTAL	% PREMIUM
Kookaburra 1 kilogram	Australia	$1,151.61	$98.22	$1,249.83	8.53%
10 oz. bar	Johnson Matthey	$358.20	$40.44	$398.64	11.29%
100 oz. bar	Johnson Matthey	$3,582.00	$172.17	$3,754.17	4.81%
100 oz. bar	Royal Canadian Mint	$3,582.00	$195.28	$3,777.28	5.45%
PLATINUM					
Eagle 1 oz.	United States	$1,721.00	$258.46	$1,979.46	15.02%
Eagle 1/2 oz.	United States	$860.50	$101.12	$961.62	11.75%
Eagle 1/4 oz.	United States	$430.25	$50.56	$480.81	11.75%
Eagle 1/10 oz.	United States	$172.10	$44.94	$217.04	26.11%
Maple Leaf 1 oz.	Canada	$1,721.00	$202.26	$1,923.26	11.75%
Koala 1 oz.	Australia	$1,721.00	$202.27	$1,923.27	11.75%
1 oz. bar	Credit Suisse	$1,721.00	$112.36	$1,833.36	6.53%
10 oz. bar	Pamp Suisse	$17,210.00	$1,011.36	$18,221.36	5.88%

BULLION COIN OR BAR	COUNTRY OR REFINER	VALUE OF PRECIOUS METAL	PREMIUM	TOTAL	% PREMIUM
PALLADIUM					
Maple Leaf 1 oz.	Canada	$729.00	$51.23	$780.23	7.03%
1 oz. bar	Credit Suisse	$729.00	$38.42	$767.42	5.27%
1 kilogram bar	Pamp Suisse	$23,437.35	$1,235.29	$24,672.64	5.27%

"FOR MODERN

BULLION COINAGE,

MADE FROM THE

MID-1980S UNTIL

THE PRESENT, THE

STATISTICS ARE

DEAD ON."

CHAPTER 11

Mintages for Modern Bullion Coins

The United States Mint has produced reliable minting and production statistics for more than a century. Earlier minting records, such as those suggesting that 19,000 silver dollars dated 1804 were produced, are not so reliable. For modern bullion coinage, made from the mid-1980s until the present, the statistics are dead on.

That affords a unique opportunity when someone buying bullion coin has the ability to acquire specific dates at no premium, or at a very modest premium over the applicable spot price. The reason: there are individuals who collect bullion coins by date, just as there are those who collect Lincoln cents, Roosevelt dimes or Morgan silver dollars.

The charts that follow give the mintages for the uncirculated Eagles by metal (silver, gold and platinum) and then break them down by mintage (low to high). The real surprise is how many are actually scarce coins in addition to having bullion value. At least 18 of the gold issues (mostly quarter Eagles, containing 1/4 ounce gold) have mintages of less than 100,000 coins, and about seven of the gold pieces have mintages of about 60,000 or less.

Accurate mintage figures for foreign mints are sometimes difficult to come by, but it always makes sense to check because if no numismatic premium is applied, the lower mintage coin is a better bet.

AMERICAN SILVER EAGLE MINTAGE			
YEAR	**MINTAGE**	**YEAR**	**MINTAGE** (low to high)
1986	5,393,005	1996	3,603,386
1987	11,442,334	1994	4,227,319
1988	5,004,646	1997	4,295,004
1989	5,203,327	1995	4,672,051
1990	5,840,210	1998	4,847,549
1991	7,191,066	1988	5,004,646
1992	5,540,068	1989	5,203,327
1993	6,763,762	1986	5,393,005
1994	4,227,319	1992	5,540,068
1995	4,672,051	1990	5,840,210
1996	3,603,386	1993	6,763,762
1997	4,295,004	1991	7,191,066
1998	4,847,549	1999	7,408,640
1999	7,408,640	2003	8,495,008
2000	9,239,132	2005	8,891,025
2001	9,001,711	2001	9,001,711
2002	10,539,026	2007	9,029,036
2003	8,495,008	2000	9,239,132
2004	9,617,754	2004	9,617,754
2005	8,891,025	2006	10,021,000
2006	10,021,000	2002	10,539,026
2007	9,029,036	1987	11,442,334
2008	20,583,000	2011 May	17,504,000
2009	27,138,500	2008	20,583,000
2010	34,662,500	2009	27,138,500
2011 May	17,504,000	2010	34,662,500
TOTAL	256,154,059	**TOTAL**	256,154,059

For silver Eagles, at least 10 dates are below 6 million pieces, and more than half are less than 8 million. Given that the high point in mintage is about 35 million pieces, there's some opportunity for numismatic premium in this bullion acquisition.

American Silver Eagle

CANADIAN SILVER MAPLE LEAF MINTAGE			
YEAR	MINTAGE	YEAR	MINTAGE (low to high)
1988	1,155,931	1997	100,970
1989	3,332,200	1996	250,445
1990	1,708,800	1995	326,244
1991	644,300	1992	343,800
1992	343,800	2001	398,563
1993	1,133,900	2000	403,562
1994	889,946	2002	576,196
1995	326,244	1998	591,359
1996	250,445	1991	644,300
1997	100,970	2004	680,925
1998	591,359	2003	684,750
1999	1,229,442	1994	889,946
2000	403,562	2005	955,694
2001	398,563	1993	1,133,900
2002	576,196	1988	1,155,931
2003	684,750	1999	1,229,442
2004	680,925	1990	1,708,800
2005	955,694	2006	2,464,727
2006	2,464,727	1989	3,332,200
2007	3,526,052	2007	3,526,052
2008	7,909,161	2008	7,909,161
2009	9,727,592	2009	9,727,592
2010	NA	2010	NA
2011	NA	2011	NA
TOTAL	39,034,559		

Canadian Silver Maple Leaf

AUSTRALIAN KOOKABURRA MINTAGES

YEAR	MINTAGE	YEAR	MINTAGE (low to high)
Kookaburra 1990	301,500	1999	300,000
Kookaburra 1991	300,000	1991	300,000
Kookaburra 1992	300,000	1992	300,000
Kookaburra 1993	300,000	1993	300,000
Kookaburra 1994	300,000	1994	300,000
Kookaburra 1995	300,000	1995	300,000
Kookaburra 1996	300,000	1996	300,000
Kookaburra 1997	300,000	1997	300,000
Kookaburra 1998	300,000	1998	300,000
Kookaburra 1999	300,000	2004	300,000
Kookaburra 2000	300,000	2000	300,000
Kookaburra 2001	300,000	2001	300,000
Kookaburra 2002	300,000	2002	300,000
Kookaburra 2003	300,000	2003	300,000
Kookaburra 2004	300,000	2006	300,000
Kookaburra 2005	300,000	2005	300,000
Kookaburra 2006	300,000	2007	300,000
Kookaburra 2007	300,000	2008	300,000
Kookaburra 2008	300,000	1990	301,500
Kookaburra 2009	350,000	2009	350,000
Kookaburra 2010	NA	NA	NA
TOTAL	**6,051,500**		

AUSTRALIAN KOALA

UNCIRCULATED KOALA 1/2 OZ BUILLION COINS

YEAR	MINTAGE
Koala 2008	13,994
Koala 2009	15,334
Koala 2010	NA

UNCIRCULATED KOALA 1OZ BULLION COINS

YEAR	MINTAGE
Koala 2007	137,764
Koala 2008	84,057
Koala 2009	100,000
Koala 2010	100,000

GILDED KOALA 1OZ BULLION COINS

YEAR	MINTAGE
Koala 2008	10,000
Koala 2009	10,000
Koala 2010	10,000

UNCIRCULATED KOALA 100Z BULLION COINS

YEAR	MINTAGE
Koala 2007	0
Koala 2008	4,367
Koala 2009	6,556
Koala 2010	NA

UNCIRCULATED KOALA 1 KILO BULLION COINS

YEAR	MINTAGE
Koala 2007	0
Koala 2008	13,118
Koala 2009	34,947
Koala 2010	NA

AUSTRALIAN KANGAROO MINTAGES			
YEAR	MINTAGE	YEAR	MINTAGE (low to high)
Kangaroo 1993	77,853	2008	6,802
Kangaroo 1994	47,496	2009	20,000
Kangaroo 1995	75,350	2006	25,535
Kangaroo 1996	49,398	2005	26,146
Kangaroo 1997	72,850	2002	32,376
Kangaroo 1998	49,398	2003	35,230
Kangaroo 1999	49,398	2000	42,638
Kangaroo 2000	42,638	2001	45,562
Kangaroo 2001	45,562	1994	47,496
Kangaroo 2002	32,376	1999	49,398
Kangaroo 2003	35,230	1996	49,398
Kangaroo 2004	55,057	1998	49,398
Kangaroo 2005	26,146	2004	55,057
Kangaroo 2006	25,535	1997	72,850
Kangaroo 2007	8,598	2007	75,350
Kangaroo 2008	6,802	1995	75,350
Kangaroo 2009	20,000	1993	77,853
Kangaroo 2010	NA	2010	NA
TOTAL	719,687		

Australian Kangaroo

MEXICAN LIBERTAD 1 OZ. MINTAGES			
YEAR	MINTAGE	YEAR	MINTAGE (low to high)
Libertad 1982	1,049,680	1998	67,000
Libertad 1983	1,001,768	1999	95,000
Libertad 1984	1,014,000	1997	100,000
Libertad 1985	2,017,000	2007	200,000
Libertad 1986	1,699,426	1996	300,000
Libertad 1987	500,000	2006	300,000
Libertad 1988	1,500,500	2000	340,000
Libertad 1989	1,396,500	1994	400,000
Libertad 1990	1,200,002	2004	450,000
Libertad 1991	1,650,518	1995	500,000
Libertad 1992	2,458,000	1987	500,000
Libertad 1993	1,000,000	2005	698,281
Libertad 1994	400,000	2001	725,000
Libertad 1995	500,000	2003	805,000
Libertad 1996	300,000	2002	850,000
Libertad 1997	100,000	2008	950,000
Libertad 1998	67,000	1993	1,000,000
Libertad 1999	95,000	1983	1,001,768
Libertad 2000	340,000	1984	1,014,000
Libertad 2001	725,000	1982	1,049,680
Libertad 2002	850,000	1990	1,200,002
Libertad 2003	805,000	1989	1,396,500
Libertad 2004	450,000	1988	1,500,500
Libertad 2005	698,281	2009	1,650,000
Libertad 2006	300,000	1991	1,650,518
Libertad 2007	200,000	1986	1,699,426
Libertad 2008	950,000	1985	2,017,000
Libertad 2009	1,650,000	1992	2,458,000
Libertad 2010	NA	2010	NA
		TOTAL	24,917,675

Mexican Libertad
1 oz.

MEXICAN LIBERTAD 2 OZ. MINTAGES

YEAR	MINTAGE	YEAR	MINTAGE (low to high)
Libertad 1996	50,000	2005	3,549
Libertad 1997	15,000	1999	5,000
Libertad 1998	7,000	2006	5,800
Libertad 1999	5,000	2001	6,700
Libertad 2000	7,500	1998	7,000
Libertad 2001	6,700	2000	7,500
Libertad 2002	8,700	2004	8,000
Libertad 2003	9,500	2007	8,000
Libertad 2004	8,000	2002	8,700
Libertad 2005	3,549	2003	9,500
Libertad 2006	5,800	1997	15,000
Libertad 2007	8,000	2008	17,000
Libertad 2008	17,000	2009	46,000
Libertad 2009	46,000	1996	50,000
Libertad 2010	NA	NA	NA
		TOTAL	197,749
		TOTAL OZ	395,498

MEXICAN LIBERTAD 5 OZ. MINTAGES			
YEAR	MINTAGE	YEAR	MINTAGE (low to high)
Libertad 1996	20,000	2005	2,401
Libertad 1997	10,000	1999	2,800
Libertad 1998	3,500	2006	3,000
Libertad 1999	2,800	2007	3,000
Libertad 2000	4,000	1998	3,500
Libertad 2001	4,000	2004	3,923
Libertad 2002	5,200	2001	4,000
Libertad 2003	6,000	2000	4,000
Libertad 2004	3,923	2002	5,200
Libertad 2005	2,401	2003	6,000
Libertad 2006	3,000	2008	9,000
Libertad 2007	3,000	1997	10,000
Libertad 2008	9,000	1996	20,000
Libertad 2009	21,000	2009	21,000
Libertad 2010	NA	2010	NA
		TOTAL	197,749
		TOTAL OZ	395,498
GRAND TOTAL OZ			25,802,293

CHINESE PANDA MINTAGES			
YEAR	**MINTAGE**	**YEAR**	**MINTAGE (low to high)**
Panda 1986	0	1986	0
Panda 1987	31,000	1987	31,000
Panda 1988	0	1988	0
Panda 1989	225,000	1998	100,000
Panda 1990	200,000	1996	100,000
Panda 1991	100,000	1991	100,000
Panda 1992	100,000	1992	100,000
Panda 1993	120,000	1994	100,000
Panda 1994	100,000	1993	120,000
Panda 1995	168,000	1995	168,000
Panda 1996	100,000	1990	200,000
Panda 1997	600,000	1989	225,000
Panda 1998	100,000	2001	250,000
Panda 1999	600,000	2002	500,000
Panda 2000	600,000	2000	600,000
Panda 2001	250,000	1997	600,000
Panda 2002	500,000	1999	600,000
Panda 2003	600,000	2003	600,000
Panda 2004	600,000	2004	600,000
Panda 2005	600,000	2005	600,000
Panda 2006	600,000	2006	600,000
Panda 2007	600,000	2007	600,000
Panda 2008	600,000	2008	600,000
Panda 2009	600,000	2009	600,000
Panda 2010	600,000	2010	600,000
		TOTAL	8,594,000

2011 Chinese Panda

BRITISH BRITANNIA MINTAGES			
YEAR	MINTAGE	YEAR	MINTAGE (low to high)
Britannia 1998	88,909	2001	44,816 Standing Britannia
Britannia 1999	69,394	2002	48,816 Chariot
Britannia 2000	81,301	1999	69,394 Standing Britannia
Britannia 2001	44,816	2003	73,271 Una and the Lion
Britannia 2002	48,816	2000	81,301 Standing Britannia
Britannia 2003	73,271	1998	88,909 Britannia's Helmet
Britannia 2004	100,000	2004	100,000 Standing Britannia
Britannia 2005	NA	2005	NA
Britannia 2006	100,000	2006	100,000 Standing Britannia
Britannia 2007	100,000	2007	100,000 Seated Britannia & Lion
Britannia 2008	100,000	2008	100,000 Britannia on the Beach
Britannia 2009	100,000	2009	100,000 Chariot
Britannia 2010	100,000	2010	100,000 Corinthian Helmet
Britannia 2011	100,000	2011	100,000 Billowing Union Flag
		TOTAL	8,594,000

British Britannia

The problem with analyzing gold Eagle fractionals is that many of the 1/10 ounce coins have jewelry usage; but consider the table (below) listing all of the fractional (and the 1 ounce piece) in ranked priority of mintage:

AMERICAN GOLD EAGLE MINTAGES		
2011	28,000	1/4 oz thru March only
2007	34,004	1/4 oz
1991	36,100	1/4 oz
1990	41,000	1/4 oz
2006	46,000	1/4 oz
1988	49,000	1/4 oz
1992	54,800	1/4 oz
1996	60,318	1/4 oz
1994	62,000	1/4 oz
2010	62,000	1/4 oz
2002	62,027	1/4 oz
2008	70,000	1/4 oz
1993	70,000	1/4 oz
2001	71,280	1/4 oz
2005	72,015	1/4 oz
2003	74,029	1/4 oz
2004	76,014	1/4 oz
1989	81,789	1/4 oz
1995	90,000	1/4 oz
1997	108,805	1/4 oz
2009	110,000	1/4 oz
2000	128,964	1/4 oz
2007	140,016	1/2 oz
2007	140,016	1 oz
2001	143,605	1/2 oz
2001	143,605	1 oz
2011	145,000	1/10 oz
1988	159,500	1/10 oz
1991	165,200	1/10 oz

AMERICAN GOLD EAGLE MINTAGES		
1996	189,148	1 oz
1996	189,148	1/2 oz
1994	190,000	1/10 oz
2007	190,010	1/10 oz
2006	201,500	1/2 oz
2006	201,500	1 oz
1992	207,000	1/10 oz
1990	210,210	1/10 oz
1993	215,000	1/10 oz
2002	222,029	1/2 oz
2002	222,029	1 oz
1995	226,000	1 oz
1995	226,000	1/2 oz
2002	230,027	1/10 oz
1995	232,000	1/10 oz
1991	243,100	1/2 oz
1991	243,100	1 oz
1994	243,500	1/2 oz
1994	243,500	1 oz
2011	243,500	1 oz
2011	243,500	1/2 oz
2003	245,029	1/10 oz
1989	264,790	1/10 oz
2001	269,147	1/10 oz
1987	269,255	qtr. oz
2006	270,000	1/10 oz
2009	270,000	1/10 oz
2004	275,016	1/10 oz
2005	300,043	1/10 oz
2008	305,000	1/10 oz

AMERICAN GOLD EAGLE MINTAGES		
1998	309,829	1/4 oz
1992	326,000	1 oz
1992	326,000	1/2 oz
2005	356,555	1 oz
2005	356,555	1/2 oz
1990	373,210	1 oz
1990	373,210	1/2 oz
2010	390,080	1/10 oz
1996	401,964	1/10 oz
1989	415,790	1/2 oz
1989	415,790	1 oz
2003	416,032	1/2 oz
2003	416,032	1 oz
2000	433,319	1/2 oz
2000	433,319	1 oz
2004	437,019	1 oz
2004	437,019	1/2 oz
1993	439,000	1 oz
1993	439,000	1/2 oz
1988	465,000	1/2 oz
1988	465,000	1 oz
1997	528,266	1/10 oz
1999	564,232	1/4 oz

AMERICAN GOLD EAGLE MINTAGES		
2000	569,153	1/10 oz
1987	580,266	1/10 oz
1997	665,508	1/2 oz
1997	665,508	1 oz
2008	710,000	1 oz
2008	710,000	1/2 oz
1986	726,031	1/4 oz
1986	912,609	1/10 oz
1987	1,045,500	1/2 oz
1987	1,045,500	1 oz
2010	1,143,000	1 oz
2010	1,143,000	1/2 oz
2009	1,176,000	1/2 oz
2009	1,176,000	1 oz
1998	1,344,520	1/10 oz
1986	1,362,650	1 oz
1986	1,362,650	1/2 oz
1998	1,468,530	1/2 oz
1998	1,468,530	1 oz
1999	1,505,027	1 oz
1999	1,505,027	1/2 oz
1999	2,750,338	1/10 oz

1 oz. American Gold Eagle

½ oz. American Gold Eagle

¼ oz. American Gold Eagle

MINTING STATISTICS

The minting statistics from which these are derived are found in this table that is useful both as a checklist and for mintage purposes.

GOLD EAGLES BY YEAR				
	Gold 1 Ounce	Gold ½ Ounce	Gold 1/4 Ounce	Gold 1/10 Ounce
1986	1,362,650	1,362,650	726,031	912,609
1987	1,045,500	1,045,500	269,255	580,266
1988	465,000	465,000	49,000	159,500
1989	415,790	415,790	81,789	264,790
1990	373,210	373,210	41,000	210,210
1991	243,100	243,100	36,100	165,200
1992	326,000	326,000	54,800	207,000
1993	439,000	439,000	70,000	215,000
1994	243,500	243,500	62,000	190,000
1995	226,000	226,000	90,000	232,000
1996	189,148	189,148	60,318	401,964
1997	665,508	665,508	108,805	528,266
1998	1,468,530	1,468,530	309,829	1,344,520
1999	1,505,027	1,505,027	564,232	2,750,338
2000	433,319	433,319	128,964	569,153
2001	143,605	143,605	71,280	269,147
2002	222,029	222,029	62,027	230,027

GOLD EAGLES BY YEAR

	Gold 1 Ounce	Gold ½ Ounce	Gold 1/4 Ounce	Gold 1/10 Ounce
2003	416,032	416,032	74,029	245,029
2004	437,019	437,019	76,014	275,016
2005	356,555	356,555	72,015	300,043
2006	201,500	201,500	46,000	270,000
2007	140,016	140,016	34,004	190,010
2008	710,000	710,000	70,000	305,000
2009	1,176,000	1,176,000	110,000	270,000
2010	1,143,000	1,143,000	62,000	390,080
2011	243,500	243,500	28,000	145,000
TOTAL MINTAGE	14,590,538	14,590,538	3,357,492	11,620,168
TOTAL OUNCES	14,590,538	7,295,269	839,373	1,162,017
ALL OUNCES	23,887,197			

MINTING BY WEIGHT

Again, for the convenience of the reader and the researcher, the mintage figures (high-low) by weight (U.S. gold Eagle – 1 ounce, 1/2 ounce, 1/4 ounce and 1/10 ounce) are compiled and included:

OUNCE		1/2 Oz		1/4 OZ		1/10 OZ	
2007	140,016	2007	140,016	2011	28,000	2011	145,000
2001	143,605	2001	143,605	2007	34,004	1988	159,500
1996	189,148	1996	189,148	1991	36,100	1991	165,200
2006	201,500	2006	201,500	1990	41,000	1994	190,000
2002	222,029	2002	222,029	2006	46,000	2007	190,010
1995	226,000	1995	226,000	1988	49,000	1992	207,000
1991	243,100	1991	243,100	1992	54,800	1990	210,210
1994	243,500	1994	243,500	1996	60,318	1993	215,000
2011	243,500	2011	243,500	1994	62,000	2002	230,027
1992	326,000	1992	326,000	2010	62,000	1995	232,000
2005	356,555	2005	356,555	2002	62,027	2003	245,029
1990	373,210	1990	373,210	2008	70,000	1989	264,790
1989	415,790	1989	415,790	1993	70,000	2001	269,147

OUNCE		1/2 Oz		1/4 OZ		1/10 OZ	
2003	416,032	2003	416,032	2001	71,280	2006	270,000
2000	433,319	2000	433,319	2005	72,015	2009	270,000
2004	437,019	2004	437,019	2003	74,029	2004	275,016
1993	439,000	1993	439,000	2004	76,014	2005	300,043
1988	465,000	1988	465,000	1989	81,789	2008	305,000
1997	665,508	1997	665,508	1995	90,000	2010	390,080
2008	710,000	2008	710,000	1997	108,805	1996	401,964
1987	1,045,500	1987	1,045,500	2009	110,000	1997	528,266
2010	1,143,000	2010	1,143,000	2000	128,964	2000	569,153
2009	1,176,000	2009	1,176,000	1987	269,255	1987	580,266
1986	1,362,650	1986	1,362,650	1998	309,829	1986	912,609
1998	1,468,530	1998	1,468,530	1999	564,232	1998	1,344,520
1999	1,505,027	1999	1,505,027	1986	726,031	1999	2,750,338

"YOU MAY NOT BE
ABLE TO GO TO THE
GROCERY STORE
AND BUY FOOD
WITH IT, BUT IF THE
WORLD'S CURRENCY
SUFFERED FROM A
SERIOUS MALADY, IT
COULD BECOME AN
ALTERNATIVE ON
SHORT NOTICE."

CHAPTER 12

Ingots are a Popular Bullion Choice

Gold is processed into one of two unit types: coins or ingots, (ingots are more commonly known as bars). The coins can be for circulation (principally 19th and early 20th century), for investment (gold American Eagle, Krugerrand, Canadian Maple Leaf), for collectors (proof coins, commemorative, and other non-circulating legal tender coinage) or as an alternative currency system to be used as being near-money. You may not be able to go to the grocery store and buy food with it, but if the world's currency suffered from a serious malady, it could

1 ounce silver ingot from APMEX

Perth Mint 1 ounce ingot (2011)

become an option on short notice.

The other alternative is ingots, which can come in all shapes and sizes. Most are stamped with the weight of the ingot, its fineness and sometimes its value. Ingots out of the Old West are known to have been stamped into it a face value – easy to do when gold's price had been fixed at $20.67 an ounce for many years, harder today.

Ingots are made commercially in 1 troy ounce units, in fractional sizes, and in much larger units intended to convey a larger storehouse of value.

Ingots tend to be individually fabricated, each is separately assayed and hallmarked, and when removed from an approved storage facility, generally find themselves in the same situation to re-enter the "warehouse receipt" marketplace.

Several years ago, I had the occasion on behalf of a client who had a large holding of gold (over 50,000 ounces in approved commodity exchange vaults) to examine the warehouse receipts for the physical gold ingots. The "perfect" specification for the ingot would have been 100 troy ounces that were .995 fine or better, each being identical.

Anecdotally, this was not really what was expected. Here's a brief summary as to the degree of variation:

CHARACTERISTIC	MEASUREMENT	NOTATIONS
Highest weight	104.88	
Lowest weight	94.828	Apparently out of conformity
Highest minimum fineness	0.9999	SCOTIA-Mocatta
Lowest minimum finest	0.995	

This turns out to be barely in conformity with New York Mercantile Exchange Rules. The applicable rule says the seller must deliver 100 troy ounces of refined gold, assaying not less than .995 fineness, cast either in one bar or in three 1 kilogram bars by an approved refiner. The weight, fineness, bar number and identifying stamp of the refiner must be clearly incised on each bar by the approved refiner.

With the gold safely in the warehouse of an approved vault for storage, the warehouse receipt for it can be traded or exchanged, just like a physical ingot. The warehouse receipt is portable, and so long as the physical asset stays in an approved depository, it does not have to be re-assayed. The stamped weight and fineness also assist in utilizing the locked-in value of the precious metal. (It is a little hard to get "change," however.)

A 100-troy ounce ingot or bar has an ever-changing value (about $150,000), but there are also many 1 ounce, 5-ounce and other sized bars not necessarily intended for trading (they do not conform), but making "change" quite easy.

"THE PRICES OF
THESE METALS
(ESPECIALLY FOR
GOLD) ARE SET
THROUGH A
REGULAR 'AUCTION'
CALLED THE DAILY
LONDON FIX."

CHAPTER 13

Methods of Investing in Gold and Precious Metals

Essentially, investors can acquire precious metals in four basic forms:

- Bullion coins
- Ingots
- Bulk coins
- Individual coins

Bullion ingots vs. bullion coins

Bullion ingots are the right way for some investors to go. Bullion coins may be the right way for others. Ingots are not a legal tender but once assayed, they can be easily transferred, if kept in safe storage. There is also a large network of commodity dealers who make a market based on ingots. The prices of these metals (especially for gold) are set through a regular "auction" called the daily "London fix."

Molten metal is ready for transfer into an ingot mold at the Perth Mint. Photo by Kathy Ganz.

HERE ARE SOME OF THE BENEFITS ASSOCIATED WITH INGOT PURCHASE OVER BULLION COINAGE:

- Usually does not disclose country of origin (legal tender Krugerrands were once banned from American import)
- Available in large sizes, anywhere from 1 ounce to a kilogram (1,000 grams)
- Easy storage in approved vaults
- Insurable
- Transportable with (usually) no customs duties in large quantities
- Generally no sales tax on investment quantities (some states)
- Generally not subject to all of the same issues of §401(m) of the Internal Revenue Code

- Gold bullion ingots are valued according to real-time markets, and the price is driven by clear and defined economic factors
- You can own precious metals, usually gold, using an unallocated pool program
- Some companies may also offer allocated programs that could often include a storage fee

HERE ARE SOME OF THE BENEFITS ASSOCIATED WITH LEGAL TENDER (NON-CIRCULATING) BULLION COINAGE:

- Legal tender coinage generally is exempt from most disclosure laws
- The size, quantity, weight and value is standardized. Typically there is no requirement to be assayed in order to buy or sell
- The weight, purity and fineness of the precious metal is guaranteed by the issuing government
- Generally, there are no counterfeits due to the rigourous enforcement of federal laws
- Large market of dealers buying and selling
- Generally not subject to customs duties
- Generally not subject to NAFTA fees on shipments to Canada
- Usually more liquid than bullion
- Gold and silver Eagles can be put in IRAs (self-directed)
- Coins are effortlessly obtained and have virtually nonexistent purchasing and selling costs
- The potential benefit of numismatic value

THE LONDON GOLD FIX

For almost a hundred years, since September 1919, the price of gold has been set, or "fixed" in the language of the proceeding, influencing the world of finance and, incidentally, the precious metal that is a part of it.

It is dominated by four market makers: The Bank of Nova Scotia-ScotiaMocatta, Deutsche Bank AG, HSBC Bank USA London Branch and Société Générale. There was a fifth member until 2004: N.M. Rothschild & Sons.

Rothschild's was established in New Court, on St. Swithin's Lane by Nathan Mayer Rothschild in 1809. On his death in 1836, it became N.M. Rothschild & Sons. By 1840, the company had become bullion broker to the Bank of England, and a dozen years later, in 1852, it took the lease of the Royal Mint Refinery.

By 1919, Rothschild had become permanent chairman of the Gold Fixing on its establishment. The fix is the procedure by which the price of gold is determined twice each business day on the London market by the five members of The London Gold Market Fixing, Ltd.

It sets a price for settling contracts of the London bullion market, but the "fix" pegs a benchmark for pricing the majority of gold products throughout the world's markets. The gold fix is conducted in United States dollars (U.S. $), pound sterling (G.B.P., or £), and the euro (€) daily at 10:30 a.m. and 3 p.m., London time, via a dedicated telephone conference facility.

The original members were N.M. Rothschild & Sons, Mocatta & Goldsmid, Pixley & Abell, Samuel Montagu & Co. and Sharps Wilkins. On Sept. 14, 1919, the gold price was fixed at £4.18s.9d (£4.9375 or 4 pounds, 18 shillings and 9 pence). The New York gold price was U.S. $20.67. The earliest of the fixings were conducted by telephone until the members started meeting at the Rothschild offices in New Court, St. Swithin's Lane. The market suspended from 1939 to 1954 because of the war and government controls.

In 1968 the London Gold pool collapsed, and then the price was fixed only once a day. Later, a second fixing was introduced at 3 p.m. to coincide with the opening of the U.S. markets. In 2004, the price of gold was no longer managed by the Bank of England - as a result N.M Rothschild left the pool. In May 5, 2004, the "fix" started to take place via a dedicated telephone conferencing system.

A tradition of the London gold fixing was that participants could raise a small Union Flag on their desk to pause proceedings. Under the telephone fixing system, participants can register a pause by saying the word "flag," and the chair ends the meeting with the phrase "There are no flags, and we're fixed."

The fix price is published widely in newspapers, on the internet and on teletext services, and is a good guide to the value of gold at that instant. You can see it on the London Bullion Market Association website, www.lbma.org.uk, and at www.wgc.net.

Martyn Whitehead, director of commodities at Barclays Capital and vice chairman of the London Bullion Market Association says, "Normally it's a 10- or 15-minute process, but it can take up to half an hour. The longest fixing actually took place back on 19th October 1987 - Black Monday. The London Gold Fix took two hours and 15 minutes to reach agreement that day." That was the day when the U.S. stock market dropped 23 percent of its value.

"Bullion bars and coins are easily purchased over the Internet…"

CHAPTER 14

Where to Buy Gold and Precious Metals

There are three channels of distribution and sales of gold and precious metals, similar to the retail distribution channels in other retail products.

1. Over-the-counter retail outlets.

In the United States, bullion bars and coins can be purchased from most of the approximately 10,000 retail coin dealers. Generally, the local coin dealers are individually owned and operated stores in strip malls and other retail locations and along with the gold and precious metals, offer rare and collectible coins and possibly rare stamps and other collectibles. Because the local coin dealer serves an area and population that is geographically limited, the local coin dealer has a limit on the total annual sales volume and accordingly, maintains inventory and availability only meet that limited demand.

2. Telemarketing retailers

Bullion bars and coins can be purchased from a number of telemarketers who offer 800 toll-free inbound call service. These telemarketers are generally larger than any of the local coin dealers since the telemarketers serve a U.S. national market and are not limited to a local geography. Larger inventories can be more efficiently managed and deliveries are generally completed using common carriers such as the U.S. Postal Service, United Parcel Service and Federal Express. Because of the investment capital required for the larger inventories, there are very few effective and successful telemarketers of bullion bars and coins.

3. Internet retailers

Since approximately 2000, Internet retailing has become one of the most preferred methods of purchasing products. Some retail products are more easily sold over the Internet, especially hard goods that do not require sizing and a personal fit. Bullion bars and coins are easily purchased over the Internet, just as easily as books, DVDs, CDs and even stocks and bonds. Internet retailers are open 24/7/365 providing added convenience and security to purchasing bullion bars and coins. Because of the technology, Internet retailers generally offer products at lower cost and more efficiently than either the over-the-counter retailers or the telemarketing retailers.

In order to easily compare the benefits of purchasing bullion bars and coins I have prepared a list of key considerations and tables of comparisons for each of the key considerations. Here is a list of those key considerations: Convenience, Support, Pricing, Transparency, Service and Selection. Since APMEX (www.APMEX.com) is one of the largest and most successful Internet retailers, I have constructed the tables of comparisons using APMEX as compared to other coin dealers, whether over-the-counter or telemarketers.

Table A. Comparison of Convenience of APMEX to Other Dealers.

CONVENIENCE	APMEX	OTHER DEALERS
Operating hours	24/7/365	Usually Monday- Friday, 8-5
Purchasing times	Includes weekends	Mostly closed on weekends
Pricing	Instantly available online	Perhaps requires multiple telephone calls
Price commitment	You commit online, your price is locked	Most often price locked upon delivery of good funds
Salesperson interaction	None; buy online without any interaction	Most often speak to a salesperson
Secure delivery	To your doorstep	Often pickup at dealer or ship
Mobile site	Buy on your smartphone	Virtually no access

Table B. Comparison of Support of APMEX to Other Dealers.

SUPPORT	APMEX	OTHER DEALERS
Account managers	Optional; Salaried with management bonus	Often required; commissioned sales
Education/ information	Daily commentary; open, mid-day, close	Perhaps some communication
Chat online for quick answers	Instantly available online, business hours	Perhaps available
Periodic market updates	Optional email with market updates and video explanation	Perhaps available
Periodic special offerings	Optional email with special opportunities	Perhaps available

Table C. Comparison of Pricing of APMEX to Other Dealers.

PRICING	APMEX	OTHER DEALERS
Sourcing of product	Authorized purchaser direct from world mints and refiners	Most often buy from the wholesalers
Pricing	Price listed online is price paid; no commissions	Most often telephone calls or multiple visits to obtain pricing
Discounts	Volume discounts	Perhaps negotiated discounts
Spot pricing	Spot pricing based on feed from exchange, updated every 60 seconds	Often different dealers have different spot prices

Table D. Comparison of Transparency of APMEX to Other Dealers.

TRANSPARENCY	APMEX	OTHER DEALERS
Buy prices	Buy prices posted online and real time on most products	Call to obtain buy prices; perhaps multiple calls required
Spread between buy and sell	Buy and sell prices on most products posted on the same page online	Often challenging to obtain the buy price when you are seeking selling prices in order to know the spread

Table E. Comparison of Service of APMEX to Other Dealers.

SERVICE	APMEX	OTHER DEALERS
Testimonials	Hundreds of testimonials posted online	Challenging to hear from other customers
Facebook	Over 20,000 Like and active chat all day	Limited Facebook presence
Customer surveys	94%-95% of customers respond "Yes" to question: "Will you refer friends and family to purchase product(s) from APMEX?"	No data

Table F. Comparison of Selection of APMEX to Other Dealers.

SELECTION	APMEX	OTHER DEALERS
Number of choices	Over 3,500 different items; thousands more when including numismatics	Usually a few hundred at the most; possibly thousands more when including numismatics
Examples	Gold- 22 classifications of product; Silver- 30 classifications of product; Platinum- 8 classifications of product; Palladium- 5 classifications of product; plus numismatics	No data

"TODAY'S INVESTOR

HAS AN ABUNDANT

CHOICE OF BULLION

PRODUCTS TO

INCLUDE IN AN

IRA, WHETHER

THEY BE COINS,

ROUNDS OR BARS."

CHAPTER 15

Bullion can be Part of Individual Retirement Accounts

Retirement assets in the United States total $17.5 trillion, according to the 2010 official Statistical Abstract of the United States. Of that amount, $4.7 trillion is in Individual Retirement Accounts with $3.056 trillion in 401(k) accounts, most of this (48%) in mutual funds. Bullion and bullion coins constitute a very small percentage (5%), which includes other non-traditional investments. However, 5% of $17.5 trillion is about $875 billion and under almost any analysis this is a substantial amount allocated to a class that includes bullion and bullion coins

Today's investor has an abundant choice of bullion products to include in

1 ounce silver American Eagle

1 ounce gold American Buffalo

HOUSEHOLDS INVESTED THEIR IRAS IN MANY TYPES OF ASSETS

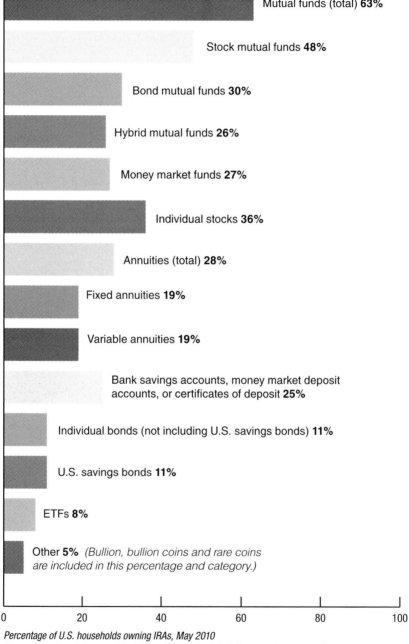

Mutual funds (total) **63%**

Stock mutual funds **48%**

Bond mutual funds **30%**

Hybrid mutual funds **26%**

Money market funds **27%**

Individual stocks **36%**

Annuities (total) **28%**

Fixed annuities **19%**

Variable annuities **19%**

Bank savings accounts, money market deposit
accounts, or certificates of deposit **25%**

Individual bonds (not including U.S. savings bonds) **11%**

U.S. savings bonds **11%**

ETFs **8%**

Other **5%** *(Bullion, bullion coins and rare coins
are included in this percentage and category.)*

0   20   40   60   80   100

Percentage of U.S. households owning IRAs, May 2010
Source: Investment Company Fact Book of 2011; Statistical Abstract of the United States.

an IRA, whether they be coins, rounds or bars.

The benefits of buying gold or other precious metals for your self-directed IRA are real. An outright investment in U.S. gold, silver or platinum Eagles may reap rewards in the years ahead.

You can use your IRA to acquire precious metals for far less than you can make the purchase in a straight over-the-counter transaction for your own account or portfolio.

The reason: when you make a contribution to your IRA, you are deferring tax on a portion of your income. Deferred compensation means that it isn't taxed now, but rather is taxed when it is withdrawn, typically as part of an actuarially sound plan after a person reaches retirement age. The tax is paid on the sum withdrawn based on then-current tax rates.

Just how much you can contribute to an IRA varies based on your age. If you are below age 50, it's $5,000; if you are above age 50, you can catch up with $6,000.

MARGINAL TAX RATES FOR 2011

You can use these tax rates to figure out how much tax you will save by increasing your deductions. A taxpayer earning $90,000, for example, is in the 25% tax bracket, for example, and will save 25 cents in federal tax for every dollar spent on a tax-deductible expense, such as mortgage interest or charity, or to the extent permitted, IRAs.

MARRIED INDIVIDUALS FILING JOINT RETURNS AND SURVIVING SPOUSES	
IF TAXABLE INCOME IS:	THE TAX IS:
Not over $17,000	10% of the taxable income
Over $17,000 but not over $69,000	$1,700 plus 15% of the excess over $17,000
Over $69,000 but not over $139,350	$9,500 plus 25% of the excess over $69,000
Over $139,350 but not over $212,300	$27,087.50 plus 28% of the excess over $139,350
Over $212,300 but not over $379,150	$47,513.50 plus 33% of the excess over $212,300
Over $379,150	$102,574 plus 35% of the excess over $379,150

Source: Internal Revenue Service, Revenue Procedure 2011-12. The IRS recommends its free Publication 590, Individual Retirement Arrangements (IRAs) for additional information. (www.irs.gov)

SILVER & GOLD AVERAGE PRICE PER YEAR

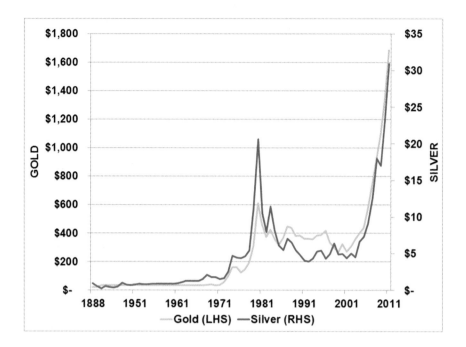

Gold (LHS) —Silver (RHS)

So, if you and your spouse earn $90,000 and buy gold totaling $5,000 for your IRA, the effective cost of the gold (at your marginal tax rate) is $3,750 (the government is your partner on the difference). This is true for all precious metals that are bullion, and many bullion coins, that you put in your IRA.

Your Existing IRA and Bullion Coins and Bars

IRAs are self directed by their very nature, which means that you as the owner of the IRA can direct the investments are you see fit. The only limitations on your investments are first imposed by your Administrator or Custodian based on the types of assets they administer or allow in accordance with their contracts and documentation. The second limitation is under the laws of the United States with respect to the types of assets that you are permitted to hold in your IRA.

Precious metals, including gold, silver, platinum and palladium, are permitted in IRAs according to U.S. law and there is a table starting on page 155 describing some of the specific metals and forms (coin or bar) that are offered by www.APMEX.com on their website.

With respect to Administrators and Custodians, there are a number of organizations that have a contract or document structure that allow the IRA owner the flexibility to acquire precious metals as permitted by U.S. law. You can access a list at www.APMEX.com/GoldinIRA/Default.aspx and see several companies that provide this service.

If your current Administrator or Custodian does not have the contracts or documents that allow you to make the investment in precious metals, then you can transfer your IRA from your current Administrator or Custodian to a replacement. All you need to do is contact the replacement Administrator or Custodian and follow their directions. You can transfer all types of IRAs, including the Standard IRA, Roth IRA and SEP IRA,

You can also rollover an IRA (all types are eligible) if you have an IRA that may be terminating as a result of a job change or other change in status. All you need to do is contact the replacement Administrator or Custodian and follow their directions.

Establishing a New IRA to Include Bullion Coins and Bars

It is easy to establish a new IRA that would include bullion bars and coins. You simply need to choose an Administrator or Custodian (there is a convenient list of options at www.APMEX.com/GoldinIRA/Default.aspx), contact your choice and follow their directions. You can establish a new IRA with your initial investment subject only to the annual contributions. Under current U.S. law, these limits are $5,000 if you are under 50 years old, $6,000 if you are over 50 years old, $10,000 for a couple under 50 years old and $12,000 for couples over 50 years old. You can have more than one IRA but the annual contributions are limited as shown above to all IRAs that you own.

Permitted Bullion Coins and Bars in Your IRA

Here is a table of precious metals products that are permitted to be included in your IRA and that are available on www.APMEX.com. The

specific list is available with images at www.APMEX.com/Category/476/
IRA_Products.aspx and the table includes all of the products with brief
descriptions as follows:

GOLD APPROVED FOR INVESTMENT BY INDIVIDUAL RETIREMENT ACCOUNTS	
ITEM	DESCRIPTION
1 Oz. Gold American Eagle	Usual production from the U.S. Mint
½ Oz. Gold American Eagle	Usual production from the U.S. Mint
¼ Oz. Gold American Eagle	Usual production from the U.S. Mint
1/10 Oz. Gold American Eagle	Usual production from the U.S. Mint
1 Oz. Gold Buffalo	Usual production from the U.S. Mint
1 Oz. Gold Canadian Maple Leaf	Usual production from the Royal Canadian Mint
½ Oz. Gold Canadian Maple Leaf	Usual production from the Royal Canadian Mint
¼ Oz. Gold Canadian Maple Leaf	Usual production from the Royal Canadian Mint
1/10 Oz. Gold Canadian Maple Leaf	Usual production from the Royal Canadian Mint
1 Oz. Gold Austrian Philaharmonic	Usual production from the Austrian Mint
½ Oz. Gold Austrian Philaharmonic	Usual production from the Austrian Mint

GOLD APPROVED FOR INVESTMENT BY INDIVIDUAL RETIREMENT ACCOUNTS

ITEM	DESCRIPTION
1 Oz. Gold American Eagle	Usual production from the U.S. Mint
½ Oz. Gold American Eagle	Usual production from the U.S. Mint
¼ Oz. Gold American Eagle	Usual production from the U.S. Mint
1/10 Oz. Gold American Eagle	Usual production from the U.S. Mint
1 Oz. Gold Buffalo	Usual production from the U.S. Mint
1 Oz. Gold Canadian Maple Leaf	Usual production from the Royal Canadian Mint
½ Oz. Gold Canadian Maple Leaf	Usual production from the Royal Canadian Mint
¼ Oz. Gold Canadian Maple Leaf	Usual production from the Royal Canadian Mint
1/10 Oz. Gold Canadian Maple Leaf	Usual production from the Royal Canadian Mint
1 Oz. Gold Austrian Philaharmonic	Usual production from the Austrian Mint
½ Oz. Gold Austrian Philaharmonic	Usual production from the Austrian Mint
¼ Oz. Gold Austrian Philaharmonic	Usual production from the Austrian Mint
1/10 Oz. Gold Austrian Philaharmonic	Usual production from the Austrian Mint
1 Gram Pamp Suisse Gold Bar (.9999)	Produced by the Pamp Suisse Refiner
2.5 Gram Pamp Suisse Gold Bar (.9999)	Produced by the Pamp Suisse Refiner
5 Gram Pamp Suisse Gold Bar (.9999)	Produced by the Pamp Suisse Refiner
10 Gram Pamp Suisse Gold Bar (.9999)	Produced by the Pamp Suisse Refiner

GOLD APPROVED FOR INVESTMENT BY INDIVIDUAL RETIREMENT ACCOUNTS	
ITEM	DESCRIPTION
1 Oz. Pamp Suisse Gold Bar (.9999)	Produced by the Pamp Suisse Refiner
100 Gram Pamp Suisse Gold Bar (.9999)	Produced by the Pamp Suisse Refiner
5 Oz. Pamp Suisse Gold Bar (.9999)	Produced by the Pamp Suisse Refiner
10 Oz. Pamp Suisse Gold Bar (.9999)	Produced by the Pamp Suisse Refiner
1 Gram Statue of Liberty Credit Suisse Gold Bar (.9999)	Produced by the Credit Suisse Refiner
2 Gram Statue of Liberty Credit Suisse Gold Bar (.9999)	Produced by the Credit Suisse Refiner
5 Gram Statue of Liberty Credit Suisse Gold Bar (.9999)	Produced by the Credit Suisse Refiner
10 Gram Statue of Liberty Credit Suisse Gold Bar (.9999)	Produced by the Credit Suisse Refiner
20 Gram Statue of Liberty Credit Suisse Gold Bar (.9999)	Produced by the Credit Suisse Refiner
1 Oz. Credit Suisse Gold Bar (.9999)	Produced by the Credit Suisse Refiner
5 Gram Perth Mint Gold Bar (.9999)	Produced by the Perth Mint
10 Gram Perth Mint Gold Bar (.9999)	Produced by the Perth Mint
20 Gram Perth Mint Gold Bar (.9999)	Produced by the Perth Mint
1 Oz. Perth Mint Gold Bar (.9999)	Produced by the Perth Mint
10 Oz. Perth Mint Gold Bar (.9999)	Produced by the Perth Mint
1 Oz. Johnson Matthey Gold Bar (.9999)	Produced by the Johnson Matthey Refiner
10 Oz. Johnson Matthey Pressed Gold Bar (.9999)	Produced by the Johnson Matthey Refiner

GOLD APPROVED FOR INVESTMENT BY INDIVIDUAL RETIREMENT ACCOUNTS

ITEM	DESCRIPTION
10 Oz. Johnson Matthey Poured Gold Bar (.9999)	Produced by the Johnson Matthey Refiner
1 Oz. Argor-Heraeus Gold Bar (.9999)	Produced by the Heraeus Refiner
1 Kilogram (32.15 Oz.) Royal Canadian Mint Gold Bar (.9999)	Produced by the Royal Canadian Mint
100 Oz. Royal Canadian Mint Gold Bar (.9999)	Produced by the Royal Canadian Mint
1 Oz. Proof Gold American Eagle	Highly polished proof production from the U.S. Mint
½ Oz. Proof Gold American Eagle	Highly polished proof production from the U.S. Mint
4 Coin Proof Gold American Eagle Set, with 1 Oz., ½ Oz., ¼ Oz, and 1/10 Oz. Coins	Highly polished proof production from the U.S. Mint

SILVER APPROVED FOR INVESTMENT BY INDIVIDUAL RETIREMENT ACCOUNTS	
ITEM	DESCRIPTION
1 Oz. Silver American Eagle	Usual production from the U.S. Mint
1 Oz. Silver Canadian Maple Leaf	Usual production from the Royal Canadian Mint
1 Oz. Silver Austrian Philaharmonic	Usual production from the Austrian Mint
1 Oz. Engelhard Silver Bar (.999)	Produced by the Engelhard Refiner
10 Oz. Engelhard Silver Bar (.999)	Produced by the Engelhard Refiner
100 Oz. Engelhard Silver Bar (.999)	Produced by the Engelhard Refiner
1 Oz. Johnson Matthey Silver Bar (.999)	Produced by the Johnson Matthey Refiner
4 Oz. Johnson Matthey Silver Bar (.999)	Produced by the Johnson Matthey Refiner
10 Oz. Johnson Matthey Silver Bar (.999)	Produced by the Johnson Matthey Refiner
1 Kilogram (32.15 Oz.) Johnson Matthey Silver Bar (.999)	Produced by the Johnson Matthey Refiner

SILVER APPROVED FOR INVESTMENT BY INDIVIDUAL RETIREMENT ACCOUNTS	
ITEM	DESCRIPTION
50 Oz. Johnson Matthey Silver Bar (.999)	Produced by the Johnson Matthey Refiner
100 Oz. Johnson Matthey Silver Bar (.999)	Produced by the Johnson Matthey Refiner
10 Oz. APMEX Silver Bar (.999)	Produced for APMEX
1 Kilogram (32.15 Oz.) APMEX Silver Bar (.999)	Produced for APMEX
100 Oz. APMEX Silver Bar (.999)	Produced for APMEX
100 Oz. Royal Canadian Mint Silver Bar (.999)	Produced by the Royal Canadian Mint
1 Oz. Proof Silver American Eagle	Highly polished proof production from the U.S. Mint

PLATINUM APPROVED FOR INVESTMENT BY INDIVIDUAL RETIREMENT ACCOUNTS	
ITEM	DESCRIPTION
1 Oz. Platinum American Eagle	Usual production from the U.S. Mint
½ Oz. Platinum American Eagle	Usual production from the U.S. Mint
¼ Oz. Platinum American Eagle	Usual production from the U.S. Mint
1/10 Oz. Platinum American Eagle	Usual production from the U.S. Mint
1 Oz. Platinum Canadian Maple Leaf	Usual production from the Royal Canadian Mint
1 Gram Johnson Matthey Platinum Bar (.999)	Produced by the Johnson Matthey Refiner
1 Oz. Pamp Suisse Platinum Bar (.999)	Produced by the Pamp Suisse Refiner
10 Oz. Pamp Suisse Platinum Bar (.999)	Produced by the Pamp Suisse Refiner
50 Oz. NYMEX deliverable Platinum Bar/Plate (.9995)	Approved Refiners and Assayers for NYMEX
1 Oz. Proof Platinum American Eagle	Highly polished proof production from the U.S. Mint

PALLADIUM APPROVED FOR INVESTMENT BY INDIVIDUAL RETIREMENT ACCOUNTS	
ITEM	DESCRIPTION
1 Oz. Palladium Canadian Maple Leaf	Usual production from the Royal Canadian Mint
1 Oz. Engelhard Palladium Bar (.999)	Produced by the Engelhard Refiner
1 Oz. Johnson Matthey Palladium Bar (.999)	Produced by the Johnson Matthey Refiner
1 Oz. Johnson Matthey Palladium Round (.999)	Produced by the Johnson Matthey Refiner
1 Oz. Pamp Suisse Palladium Bar (.999)	Produced by the Pamp Suisse Refiner
10 Oz. Pamp Suisse Palladium Bar (.999)	Produced by the Pamp Suisse Refiner
1 Kilogram Pamp Suisse Palladium Bar (.999)	Produced by the Pamp Suisse Refiner

"What's happened
with silver
is something
that is more
akin to Butch
Cassidy and the
Sundance Kid."

CHAPTER 16

Putting it All in Perspective

John Maynard Keynes (1883-1946), the British economist who helped create the postwar international monetary system with its re-emphasis on precious metals, claimed in *Monetary Reform* (1924) that "the gold standard is already a barbarous relic." If this statement would have been true, in the nearly 90 years since then, gold's moment should have passed, the luster of silver should have faded when it was removed from coinage, and platinum and palladium should be relegated to auto emission catalysts.

However, the precious metal moment has lasted longer than anyone suspected, least of all Keynes, but instead of being consigned to the dust bin of history, gold has continued as king, and silver's price is so pressing that the U.S. Mint has had to reprice some major products intended for collectors. Even platinum's luster has a sheen to it, and there is every expectation that the Congressionally mandated palladium bullion coin will score a home run.

A 1/2 ounce gold Krugerrand

Silver bars and coins from around the world.

Gold has gone from $20.67 at the start of the 20th century to $35 an ounce at the time of FDR. It took two Nixon devaluations in 1971 and 1973 to bring the "official price" to $42.22, even though the free market price is more than 40 times what the accountants and government bankers with the green eye shades says it is worth.

That's a distinction that Maynard Keynes would have appreciated.

What's happened with silver is something that is more akin to Butch Cassidy and the Sundance Kid. It jumped in the mid-1930s and seems unready to retreat – yet some involved in this market send mixed messages, trying to squeeze out a 25-cent an ounce gain.

But silver remains active, on the move, and is now featured in jewelry as well as bullion coins– not to mention a number of U.S. Mint products that have a major input into the marketplace.

Platinum and palladium enter this mix as precious metals and rare in the earth, but with more of an industrial than monetary use.

A 1 ounce .99999 gold Maple Leaf

A 1 ounce silver Chinese Panda

And even as gold has displaced platinum as the most valuable precious metal per ounce, there is uniformity in most circles in believing that in the long term, these precious metals will have continuing vitality.

Putting this all in perspective, the vitality of the precious metals market remains strong. Just look at the Mint's product line, the cost, and the number of orders. A 25-year celebration set for the anniversary of the American eagle sold out in a mere three hours. Even bullion coins are starting to become collectible items in their own right.

In the last three years alone (2009, 2010 and 2011), more than 75 million ounces of silver eagles bullion coins have been produced by the U.S. Mint for sale; more than 23 million ounces of gold eagle bullion coins were produced. Even platinum is a success that palladium will bring to a new level.

It's all because Americans have become enamored with precious metals.

A 2006 gold American Eagle

Glossary

ACCELERATED SUPPLY: Precious metal which has not yet been produced, but is anticipated due to forward sales from mines.

ACCEPTABLE: Precious metal production by refiners or assayers who are known to the London market as producers of good delivery bars.

ACID TEST: Determination of precious metal fineness by observation of its reaction to certain acid solutions.

ACTUAL GOLD CONTENT: The weight of pure gold remaining after any alloys have been separated out of it.

AD VALOREM: According to value – the levy of fees or duty based upon a metal's selling price.

AG: Chemical symbol for silver.

AGW: Actual gold weight.

ALIQUOT: A representative sample taken from a precious metals bar for assay to determine the bar's fine gold content.

ALLOCATED: Metal inventory which is designated as belonging to a particular owner/secured creditor.

ALLOY: A mixture of two or more chemical elements, at least one of which is a metal.

ALLUVIAL GOLD: Small particles of gold which have been washed out of veins or loads and can be found loose on the surface, typically from a former river bed.

AP: Authorized Purchaser (AP) of United States Mint bullion coins or approved in writing by the United States Mint to be placed on the United States Mint bullion retail list at www.usmint.gov/bullionretailer.

ASSAY: The determination of the precious metal content of an ore, bullion or alloy.

AU: The chemical symbol for gold.

AVOIRDUPOIS: System of weights based on the 16 ounce pound; normally not used for precious metals.

BRITANNIA: British bullion coins minted in one troy ounce, half ounce, quarter ounce and tenth ounce sizes and fineness of .917 or 22k.

BULLION: Gold or silver of at least 99.5% purity in bar, round or ingot form.

BULLION BANK: An investment house that clears wholesale or commercial transactions in physical gold.

BULLION COIN: A legal tender coin the value of which primarily depends on its metal content rather than its numismatic value.

BUSINESS STRIKE: A coin struck for general circulation, rather than proof issues.

CARAT: A measure of the proportion of gold in an alloy: 24 carat is pure gold, often expressed as K or kt, e.g. 18K is 18/24ths or 3/4 (75%) gold.

CASH MARKET: Transactions which require delivery and payment within two business days.

CERTIFICATE: Document indicating ownership of physical metal.

CHEVRONETZ: A Russian bullion coin, 900 fine with fine gold content of 0.2489 troy ounces and a face value of 10 roubles. Issued in the 1970s.

CHUK KAM: Chinese for "pure gold" – minimum 99% purity.

CLAD COINAGE: Coins made of layers of different metals; the U.S. dime, quarter and half dollar starting in 1965. The U.S. half dollar (1965-70) is clad and 40% silver.

CLIPPING: Intentional shaving of precious metal from a coin or other bullion.

COIN GOLD: A gold alloy, usually with a minimum fine gold content of 900, used to make coins – usually in combination with silver or copper to improve durability.

CONSIGNMENT STOCKS: Gold or silver bars held against a guarantee of payment.

CORONA: "corona" Austrian gold coin (100 Corona contains .9802 tr. Oz).

CULL: Coin removed from circulation or eligible to be removed due to either wear or defect.

DELIVERY: Providing physical product of a precious metal product to its owner or assignee.

DERIVATIVE: A financial instrument, the value of which is based on an underlying asset

DORÉ: An unrefined alloy of gold with variable quantities of silver and smaller quantities of base metals, which is produced at a mine before passing on to a refinery for upgrading to London Good Delivery standard.

DOUBLE EAGLE: Gold coin with a face value of US $20 issued as legal tender in the United States during the period 1849-1933. It is 900 fine with a fine gold content of 0.9675 troy ounces.

DWT: Abbreviation for pennyweight (1/20 troy ounce, 0.05 tr. oz).

EAGLE: Named in the original Coinage Act of 1792, the earliest legal tender U.S. gold coin first minted in 1795; originally .91667 fine. Other denominations use it as a basis (half eagle = $5; double eagle = $20). The eagle's composition has been .900 fine since 1837. [check date]

FACE VALUE: the stated value (legal tender value) on a coin (i.e., one cent, 50 cents, one dollar, etc.).

FIAT MONEY: A medium of exchange which has value only because a government has declared it to be so. A fiat currency may or may not be convertible into anything of value.

FINENESS: The proportion of precious metal in an alloy expressed as parts in 1,000.

FINE OUNCE: Weight of a precious metal coin in troy ounces.

FINE WEIGHT: The weight of gold contained in a bar, coin or bullion as determined by multiplying the gross weight by the fineness.

FIRE ASSAY: The most thorough and accurate (to 1 part in 10,000) means of determining the purity of a gold bullion or ore sample. Also the most expensive and destructive assay procedure.

FIX: End of session settlement price.

FRACTIONAL: for a precious metal coin, a specimen that is part of an ounce, typically 1/20, 1/10, 1/4, and ½, though there are others.

GC: A common quote symbol for gold futures.

GOLD: A metallic element, atomic number 79.

GOLD FIXING: Price set twice each day as part of the "London Fix" in morning and afternoon.

GOLD FILLED: Jewelry made of a base metal with a gold alloy outer coating. In the US, a gold filled piece is coated with 10-18k gold comprising at least five percent of the item's total weight.

GOLD FLASHED: A gold coating of less than seven millionths of an inch in thickness – also known as gold washed.

GOLD PARITY: Legally fixed quantity of gold to which a monetary unit is pegged.

GOLD POOL: An alliance between the central banks of Britain, Belgium, France, Italy, the Netherlands, Switzerland, the United States and West Germany from 1961 to 1968 which endeavored to maintain the gold price at US $35 dollars per troy ounce.

GOLD/SILVER RATIO: The number of ounces of silver that can be bought with one ounce of gold.

GOLD STANDARD: A monetary system with a fixed price for gold, and with gold coin either forming the whole circulation of currency within a country or with notes representing and redeemable in gold.

GOLD WARRANT: A warrant giving the buyer the right to buy gold at a specific price on a specified value date, for which the buyer pays a premium. While similar in structure to options, warrants are securitized instruments.

GOOD DELIVERY BAR: A precious metal ingot which conforms to the specifications of a particular metals exchange.

GRADING: Not something that you have to worry about with many bullion products. Bullion coins are graded, however, on a verbal description of "Poor" to "Uncirculated" and on a numerical scale of 1 to 70 (with numbers 60 to 70 reserved for various gradations of uncirculated.

GRAIN: One of the earliest units of weight for gold and silver, one grain being the equivalent of one grain of wheat taken from the middle of the ear.

GRAM: Metric unit of mass equivalent to one one-thousandth of a kilogram and about 1/31 of a troy ounce (31.1035 grams per troy ounce).

GRANULES: Bullion, including its various alloys presented for sale in granulated form, often referred to as grain.

GUINEA: British gold coin with a nominal value of £1 first issued in 1663 and named after gold from Guinea in West Africa. It was unofficially revalued at 21 shillings at The Great Recoinage of 1696, a value confirmed in 1717. It has a fineness of 916.6 and a fine gold content of approximately ¼ troy ounces.

HALLMARK: A mark or number of marks made on gold, silver or platinum products, including jewelry and other fabricated items, confirming that the quality is of the fineness marked on the item.

HEDGING: The reduction of price risk to an asset by taking an opposite position in a price-correlated asset.

INGOT: A metal bar.

INTRINSIC VALUE: The value of a coin or bar based solely on the precious metals content.

K (KARAT): Measurement of gold, with one unit in 24 being equal to 1 karat, 18k being 18/24 (75% gold), and 24k being pure gold.

KILO BAR: A popular small gold bar. A one kg bar .995 fine = 31.990 troy ounces, and a 1 kg bar 999.9 fine = 32.148 troy ounces

KILOGRAM: One thousand grams or one thousandth of a metric ton.

KRUGERRAND: South African gold coin first issued in 1967 with a fineness of 916.6.

LEVERAGE: Ownership or control of an asset without payment of its full value.

LIQUIDITY: 1. The ability to convert an asset to cash 2. a market consisting of enough buyers and sellers to ensure fair and accurate transaction prices.

GOOD DELIVERY LIST: List of acceptable refiners of gold and silver whose bars meet the required standard (of fineness, weight, marks and appearance) of the particular marketplace.

LEGAL TENDER: When a government passes a law requiring its citizenry to accept a coin or paper money for all debts, public and private, and government obligations such as customs duties. When created, all American coins were and are a legal tender, except for the Trade Dollar (struck 1873 to 1885). The trade dollar did not become a legal tender until passage of the Coinage Act of 1965.

MONETIZED BULLION: Coins whose dominant precious metal value comes from its precious metal content, not bullion value. It includes such legal tender coins as the South African Krugerrands, Mexican Onzas, and Canadian Maple Leafs, and certain restrikes and demonetized coins such as the Mexican 50 pesos. It also includes certain other coins such as the U.S. double eagles, and a variety of foreign gold coins, ranging from a British Sovereign and Swiss 20-Franc coin to a variety of other issues.

MAPLE LEAF: Canadian gold coin with a fineness of 999.9 or platinum coin with a fineness of 999.5.

MELT VALUE: The intrinsic worth of the metal in a coin or alloy.

METRIC TON: The standard measure for large quantities of precious metals; equal to 1000 kilograms or 32,150.75 troy ounces.

MORGAN DOLLAR: The Morgan dollar was minted intermittently by the U.S. Mint from 1878 to 1921.

MOZ: Million ounces.

NAPOLEON: French gold coin with a face value of 20 francs, bearing a portrait of Napoleon I or Napoleon III. It had a fineness of .900 and a fine gold content of 0.1867 troy ounces.

NOMINAL VALUE: The worth of a coin or alloy as stated on the metal itself – as opposed to the melt value, the intrinsic worth of the metal.

NUMISMATICS: The study or collection of anything used as a medium of exchange – especially coins and paper money.

NUMISMATIC COINS: Coins being purchased for an investment in the coin itself, rather than primarily for its metallic content, cf. Rev. Rul. 82-166, Int. Rev. Bull. 1982-40 at 9.

OBVERSE: The front or "heads" side of a coin.

OUNCE: The standard measure for weight in the Troy system which is the international standard for precious metals. 1/12 of a Troy pound.

PANDA: Chinese gold coin of 999.9 quality, first made in 1982.

PAPER GOLD: Any form of gold ownership which does not include physical possession or delivery.

PD: Chemical symbol of Palladium (atomic number 46).

PENNYWEIGHT: (Abbreviation: 1 DWT) One twentieth of a troy ounce (1 dwt= 0.05 tr. Oz). There are 20 dwt or pennyweights in a troy ounce.

PHILHARMONIKER: Austrian gold coin of 999.9 fineness, first issued in 1989.

PHYSICALS: An actual commodity – as opposed to a derivative or paper form of ownership.

PRECIOUS METALS: Gold, silver and platinum along with the platinum group of elements: rhodium, osmium, ruthenium, palladium and iridium. Precious metals are characteristically lustrous, ductile, rare and non-reactive.

PREMIUM: 1. An amount paid over and above the prevailing market price 2. The cash price of an option.

PT: Chemical symbol for platinum.

REFINING: The separation and purification of precious metals from other metals.

REVERSE: The "tails" or back side of a coin; the other side is the "heads" or obverse.

SEIGNORAGE: (or Seigniorage) the difference between the face value and the metal content of a coin.

SMELTING: The process of melting ores or concentrates to separate out the metal content from impurities.

SOVEREIGN: British gold coin with face value of one pound sterling, a fineness of 916.6 and a fine gold content of 0.2354 troy ounces.

SPOT: Current, real-time price or market.

STANDARD BAR or INGOT: Gold bar weighing approximately 400 ounces or 12.5 kilograms and having a minimum fineness of 995 parts per 1,000 pure gold.

TAEL: Traditional Chinese unit of weight for gold or silver.

TEFRA: Tax Equity and Fiscal Responsibility Act of 1982 (TEFRA), Pub. L. 97-248 (Approved September 3, 1982).

TROY OUNCE: The traditional unit of weight used for precious metals.

TWO NINES FIVE: 0.995 fine.

VRENELI: A Swiss gold coin (20 Franc denomination) which was issued as legal tender during the years 1897-1936 and again in 1947 and 1949. Fineness of 900.

WASHINGTON QUARTERS: The Washington quarter, the present 25-cent piece issued by the United States Mint, was originally struck in 1932.

YIELD: Cash return on an asset – other than the price of the asset. Typically, interest or dividend.

Acknowledgments

Debbie Bradley, my editor, conceived this project in response to a request from me to consider several others. A bad cold at the Florida FUN show in 2011 prevented her from discussing it with me over breakfast in Tampa, but she dogged it, and by March 2011, the contract was finalized and it was off to the races. I am grateful for the fact that she has found my voice.

Thanks to Dave Harper, my longtime editor at *Numismatic News*, who was reading my "Under the Glass" column when he was still in high school and who has helped me put my columns together, as well as news stories on a variety of precious metal-related topics for many years.

In the middle of all of this, we remodeled our home's downstairs bath and a pipe broke, flooding the basement and wreaking havoc on many of my books, files and paperwork. Brett and Larry Rosen, son and father, took care of the structural damage and contents with State Farm Insurance Company, while my wife, Kathy, showed infinite patience in having portions of this manuscript and its research spread out over my first floor office and the kitchen, the Florida room and the living room.

Joe Cobb and I have known each other for more than 30 years, dating to his service as a staffer on Capitol Hill for the House Banking Committee, working for Rep. Ron Paul during his first congressional foray. Through the years, we have stayed in touch on coin and monetary issues, with Joe usually asking for a reference from my extensive (say 5,000 volume) numismatic library, and me asking for policy analysis from some obscure time period (say the year the Mint was founded) which comes from Joe's head and a lifetime of extensive reading and analysis on the subject. Joe and I corresponded a lot about the gold to silver ratio at the time the U.S. Mint was founded, and the period shortly thereafter when France tried to find the right ratio (which it did). In asking questions about Jefferson and Hamilton's views on coinage and the value of gold and silver, he forced me to re-read the classic works of these authors that I had read many years ago, and to cautiously re-evaluate what they said, how they wrote it, and their conclusions.

The Bank of Nova Scotia began sending me their pricing sheets mid-way through the 1960s. I used them for my column first, in *The Coin Shopper*, then *The Coin Collector*, as well as Krause Publication's monthly, *The Coin Collector & Shopper*. Later, I used them for my column "Under the Glass" which first ran in *Numismatic News* in the fall of 1969 and which still runs there today, having appeared in this wonderful publication edited by Dave Harper for over six decades. Price list 178 (issued in May 1970) is the last one in my collection, and is invaluable in looking at gold bullion and coin prices over the prior decade.

My dear friend Dennis Baker of NumisMedia (the price guide and online valuation service) has supplied me with prices and access to his www. numismedia.com website for many years. He has also generously, for more than a decade, been an informal advisor on pricing and generously given his time and valuations for the extended Salomon values. (Dennis does it in MS-63 and MS-65, and until now, I have kept the data but not published the "65" – but no more. The breakthrough research is due to his diligence and his supplying it, gratis, is deeply appreciated.)

Prof. Mike Duffy of the Iowa State Extension program has kept me in steady supply of the value of Iowa's choice farmland, a good point of comparison with other assets that are a storehouse of value –like gold, silver and other precious metals, and rare coins that have a bullion component (and in some cases, a whole lot more). He has been generous with his time, and estimates both for my "Under the Glass" column which has written about this regularly, and for this book. He noted that in the first quarter of 2011, Iowa farmland rose at 19 percent or more in value, and that's the measure of what other comparables must run against.

Arthur Friedberg is one of my oldest friends in the rare coin business. We both went to college in Washington, D.C., at around the same time, Arthur at George Washington University, me at Georgetown. He graduated two years before me, in 1971, and went to work for the Coin & Currency Institute, which his father, the late Robert Friedberg founded. Arthur took the publications of the institute to new levels and probably knows more about foreign gold coins than anyone alive. For more than 30 years, I have been his lawyer, and we have co-ventured together in bringing out an edition of *Modern World Coins* (by Yeoman) where Arthur supplied the real expertise and I did the contract. We also joint ventured in marketing a gold ducat in the early 1980s for s'Rijks Munt (Netherlands State Mint), and have worked together on many projects in and around the numismatic world. I was pleased that he agreed to contribute to the front matter of this book and thrilled when he caught an error in a portion of the manuscript that I sent to him to give him a feel for the book. Now he has moved to Vermont with his wife, Nancy, and we speak over the phone rather than see each other regularly. Not only is he my friend of 40 years, but he was a valuable and critical eye for this book.

Philip Diehl has been my friend since we became acquainted on the occasion of his appointment as executive deputy director of the U.S. Mint, and later director of the Mint. He and I expanded the relationship when I became ANA president and he became chair of the Citizens Commemorative Coin Advisory Committee. He and I initially disagreed on the mission of the Citizens Committee because I took a very expansive view and Philip supported the view of the Mint bureaucracy. Later, he changed his mind because "Johnny One Note" (me) wouldn't let go. After I left the Citizens Advisory committee, we worked on the incorporation of platinum into the Mint's bevy of products, and most recently, are working on the ICTA's board of directors and on other projects. I value his insight.

Back in 1960, when I first started to collect coins, my mother, Beverlee Ganz, took me to the Rockville Centre, N.Y., public library to start reading about coins. For a half century, she was among my most avid readers and supporters, and even though she did not collect coins herself, eventually became a life member of the American Numismatic Association while I served on its board of directors. Before I was working on this book, my mother suffered a heart attack in January 2010, while visiting us from her Florida home. As this book neared completion, she was confined to Amsterdam House, a New York City skilled care facility (which we used to call nursing homes), where my sister, Dr. Sandy Ganz, heads the rehabilitative medicine division (physical therapy). As my mother moved toward the final stages of her life, I saw her almost daily and she asked if I would dedicate the book to her, which I gladly told her I would. Her insistence that I read about coins as a youth made this book possible.

My wife, Kathy, is used to my writing books or very long self-contained chapters on coins, law, and other topics. This frequently involves a lot of late night writing, when the house is quiet and telephones not really in use. This book was in draft form when we left on a month-long trip to Africa in the spring of 2011, just before my mother passed on. Kathy tolerated the time that I spent editing and re-writing, as well as adding to this manuscript with typical good humor and, more importantly, the understanding that has allowed me to write more than a dozen books in the last couple of years and more than 20 books since we were married in 1996.

Some of my earliest experiences with precious metals involved Luis Vigor, then an executive vice president of MTB, whom I inevitably called for a comment to include in either my "Under the Glass" column, or for a news story. Later, I became his friend, and his lawyer, and he persuaded me, in the early 1980s, to go to a meeting called in Indianapolis by Burton S. Blumert, a New Yorker who had transplanted himself from New York to California, and who in the process more or less invented the coin dealer's teletype. (I flew to Indianapolis for a long weekend, which is how I became a founding director and general counsel of the National Association of Coin & Precious Metals Dealers.

Since the mid-1990s, by which time I was elected to the American Numismatic Association board of governors, I have been offered a slot to either run in or be appointed to, and have worked with Eloise Ullman and Diane Piret for this unique organization that works for the benefit of the coin industry as a whole. In any event, ICTA offered their assistance in helping me lock down the specifics of state sales tax exemption on the sale of coins and bullion.

Several officials at the U.S. Mint, past and present, have my gratitude. Eleonora Hayden, the Mint historian, was helpful several years before her retirement in obtaining statistics from the turn of the 20th century that I had no access to. Mrs. Hayden was with the Mint from the 1920s well into the 1970s, and if you weren't specific and asked her about "The Secretary [of the Treasury]" she was just as likely to return to you the speaker's notes with your notes marked "that Secretary disagreed," which only left you to find out which secretary in the half century that was her watch would work. But the data she provided (which I stored with attribution) made analysis in this book easy. So, too, the late Howard Johnson of the office of technology, and Dr. Alan Goldman, provided substantive analysis 40 years ago (and I still have the notes).

The Perth Mint, which we visited on our Crystal Cruise to Australia, was kind beyond words and the photo of the fiery pouring of an ingot that Kathy took is the result.

Q. David Bowers is probably the most prolific numismatic author of this or any other generation. He is also generous with his research and with permissions to use it. One of his many books is *Louis E. Eliasberg Sr.: King of Coins* (1996), which was very useful in tracing the history of acquisition of this fabulous collection. His kind permission to use photographs of Mr. Eliasberg from that book is appreciated, making for a more enjoyable experience to all readers.

Jim Halperin, Steve Ivy and Heritage have been good friends, and strong supporters, for many years (more than 30 by my count). I have served with them on corporate boards (Jim on the ANA Board, Steve on the ICTA board), and their astute comments on the marketplace and on its surrounding environs has always proved useful. Their willingness to provide photos makes this a much more pleasant book to read. Access to their web site (www. Ha.com) and pricing data has facilitated this publication. None of the coin books that I've written would have been possible without the assistance of them and their firm.

Scott Travers, the New York City coin dealer, has been my agent for a number of books (but not this one), and we have had numerous discussions about the coin market over the last 30 years.. His significant contribution to this book was a chance comment that he made a number of years ago when he commented that Saints in MS-60, MS-61 and MS-62 rarely have anything more to say than that they parallel the gold market. I viscerally disagreed, but after hours of research, and many graphs later, I concluded he was right and told him so. They also represent a great value to someone who wants to buy bullion but wants the safety that a legal tender coin provides (even if the numismatic value is, well, not a lot). That philosophy is imbued in these pages. Thanks, Scott.

The Harry Bass Foundation, founded by the late Harry Bass, is a unique treasure. It is easily accessible, a real resource for the scholar as well as the researcher, and makes viewing coins (and their write ups) easy.

David W. Akers, who cataloged the Pittman collection, is appreciated for his recollections and information on several Pittman specimens.

Harvey Stack has been gracious through the years in providing numismatic information and his firm's catalog. Who knew, when he introduced me to William Bareford in December 1978, that I would still be writing about (and using the information acquired) it more than 30 years later.

Also thanks for their astute analysis: Jim Kingsland, the books and related materials furnished through the good graces of David Sklow, Fred Lake, David Fanning and George Frederick Kolbe, and their consignors.

And thanks for the various put-together that made for a successful manuscript: Hannah Seo, Rob Pantina, Michael Kaplan, and to Mimosa Rose, who would come in and trill that it was bedtime.

When I wrote the revision to *The World of Coins and Coin Collecting* in the early 1980s, my children were young and really showed no proclivity for coin collecting, and found none of the fascination with numismatic items that I did. They're grown now and on their own, Scott (30) in the military serving as a combat engineer in Afghanistan; Elyse (26) in a masters program at N.Y.U. (social work) and Pam (24), a paralegal in Florida. Elyse recently surprised me by asking for a book about coins that she could read to try and understand my passion. Who knows where it will lead.

Photo Credits

Franklin D. Roosevelt Presidential Library
Heritage Rare Coins
Arthur L. Friedberg
Kathy Ganz
Ira Goldberg & Larry Goldberg
U.S. Mint
Burton S. Blumert
Stack's
Q. David Bowers
Library of Congress
Foto Search dot com
British Royal Mint
Michael Sedgwick
Royal Canadian Mint
U.S. Mint
Perth Mint
Royal Australian Mint
s'Rijks Munt
Casa de Moneda (Mexico)
Fabrica de Moneda y Timbre (Spain)
Jack Huggins
Central State Numismatic Society
Krause Publications
Numismatic News
David L. Ganz
Scott Travers
Taronga Zoo (Sydney, Australia)
And those unnamed individuals who either used my camera on request to take the photos I appeared in, or handed it to their companion to complete the picture.

Appendix: Mintages of U.S. Commemorative Coins

	Minted	Proof	% Proof	Unc	% Unc	in Millions Authorized	Sold Percent	Selling price
I. CHRONOLOGICAL GOLD AND SILVER COMMEMORATIVES (AND COPPER-NICKEL HALVES, TOO)								
1982 Washington 50¢	7,104,502	4,894,044	68.89%	2,210,458	31.11%	10.000	71.05%	$225
1983 Olympic $1	2,219,596	1,577,025	71.05%	642,571	28.95%	50.000	4.44%	$225
1984 $10 Olympic Gold	573,364	497,478	86.76%	75,886	13.24%	1.000	57.34%	$350
1984 Olympic $1	2,252,514	1,801,210	79.96%	451,304	20.04%	50.000	4.51%	$425
1986 Statue of Liberty $5	499,261	404,013	80.92%	95,248	19.08%	0.500	99.85%	$225
1986 Statue of Liberty 50 C	7,853,635	6,925,627	88.18%	928,008	11.82%	10.000	78.54%	$259
1986 State Library $1	7,138,273	6,414,638	89.86%	723,635	10.14%	10.000	71.38%	$225
1987 Constitution $5	865,884	651,659	75.26%	214,225	24.74%	1.000	86.59%	$259
1987 Constitution $1	3,198,745	2,747,116	85.88%	451,629	14.12%	10.000	31.99%	$225

1984 Olympics $10 Gold Eagle/ Runners

Appendix: Mintages of U.S. Commemorative Coins

I. CHRONOLOGICAL GOLD AND SILVER COMMEMORATIVES (AND COPPER-NICKEL HALVES, TOO)								
	Minted	Proof	% Proof	Unc	% Unc	in Millions Authorized	Sold Percent	Selling price
1988 Olympic $1	1,550,734	1,359,366	87.66%	191,368	12.34%	10.000	15.51%	$259
1988 Olympic $5	413,055	281,465	68.14%	131,590	5	1.000	41.31%	$225
1989 Congress $1	931,650	767,897	82.42%	163,753	17.58%	3.000	31.06%	$225
1989 Congress $5	211,589	164,690	77.83%	46,899	22.17%	1.000	21.16%	$225
1989 Congress Bicentennial 50¢	897,401	762,198	84.93%	135,203	15.07%	4.000	22.44%	$225
1990 Eisenhower $1	1,386,130	1,144,461	82.57%	241,669	17.43%	4.000	34.65%	$259
1991 Korea $1	831,537	618,488	74.38%	213,049	25.62%	1.000	83.15%	$37
1991 Mount Rushmore $1	871,558	738,419	84.72%	133,139	15.28%	2.500	34.86%	$220
1991 Mount Rushmore $5	143,950	111,991	77.80%	31,959	22.20%	0.500	28.79%	$35
1991 USO $1	446,233	321,275	72.00%	124,958	28.00%	1.000	44.62%	$34
1991 Mount Rushmore 50¢	926,011	753,257	81.34%	172,754	18.66%	2.500	37.04%	$220
1992 Columbus $5	104,065	79,734	76.62%	24,331	23.38%	0.500	20.81%	$195

Appendix: Mintages of U.S. Commemorative Coins

I. CHRONOLOGICAL GOLD AND SILVER COMMEMORATIVES (AND COPPER-NICKEL HALVES, TOO)								
	Minted	Proof	% Proof	Unc	% Unc	in Millions Authorized	Sold Percent	Selling price
1992 Columbus $1	492,252	385,290	78.27%	106,962	21.73%	4.000	12.31%	$195
1992 Columbus 50¢	525,973	390,255	74.20%	135,718	25.80%	6.000	8.77%	$35
1992 Olympic $1	688,842	503,239	73.06%	185,603	26.94%	4.000	17.22%	$185
1992 Olympic $5	104,214	76,499	73.41%	27,715	26.59%	0.500	20.84%	$37
1992 Olympic 50¢	678,484	517,318	76.25%	161,166	23.75%	6.000	11.31%	$37
1992 White House $1	498,753	375,154	75.22%	123,599	24.78%	0.500	99.75%	$37
1993 Madison $1	627,995	532,747	84.83%	95,248	15.17%	0.900	69.78%	$33
1993 Madison $5	101,928	78,654	77.17%	23,274	22.83%	0.300	33.98%	$33
1993 Madison 50¢	775,287	584,350	75.37%	190,937	24.63%	1.000	77.53%	$33
1994 Capitol Bicentennial $1	304,421	243,597	80.02%	60,824	19.98%	0.500	60.88%	$35
1994 Jefferson	599,844	332,890	55.50%	266,954	44.50%	0.600	99.97%	$37
1994 P.O.W. $1	267,800	213,900	79.87%	53,900	20.13%	0.500	53.56%	$35
1994 Vietnam $1	275,800	219,300	79.51%	56,500	20.49%	0.500	55.16%	$37
1994 Women in Military $1	259,100	207,200	79.97%	51,900	20.03%	0.500	51.82%	$195

Appendix: Mintages of U.S. Commemorative Coins

I. CHRONOLOGICAL GOLD AND SILVER COMMEMORATIVES (AND COPPER-NICKEL HALVES, TOO)								
	Minted	Proof	% Proof	Unc	% Unc	in Millions Authorized	Sold Percent	Selling price
1994 World Cup $1	656,567	577,090	87.73%	81,524	12.27%	5.000	13.13%	$37
1994 World Cup $5	112,066	89,614	79.97%	22,447	20.03%	5.000	2.24%	$37
1994 World War Ii $1	445,667	339,358	76.15%	106,309	23.85%	1.000	44.57%	$35
1994 World Cup 50	776,851	609,354	78.20%	168,208	21.80%	5.000	15.54%	$13
1994 WWII $5	90,434	66,837	73.91%	23,597	26.09%	0.300	30.14%	$35
1994 WWII 50¢	512,759	313,801	61.20%	198,958	38.80%	2.000	25.64%	$35
1995 Civil War Battle $1	101,112	55,246	54.64%	45,866	45.36%	1.000	10.11%	
1995 Civil War 50¢	434,789	322,245	74.12%	112,544	25.88%	2.000	21.74%	$13
1995 Civil War Battle $5	67,981	55,246	81.27%	12,735	18.73%	0.300	22.66%	$12
1995 Olympics $5 Runner	72,117	57,442	79.65%	14,675	20.35%	0.175	41.21%	$33
1995 Olympics Baseball 50¢	282,692	118,087	41.77%	164,605	58.23%	2.000	14.13%	$33
1995 Olympics Basketball 50¢	340,656	169,655	49.80%	171,001	50.20%	2.000	17.03%	$37
1995 Olympics Cycling $1	138,457	118,795	85.80%	19,662	14.20%	0.750	18.46%	$37

Appendix: Mintages of U.S. Commemorative Coins

I. CHRONOLOGICAL GOLD AND SILVER COMMEMORATIVES (AND COPPER-NICKEL HALVES, TOO)								
	Minted	Proof	% Proof	Unc	% Unc	in Millions Authorized	Sold Percent	Selling price
1995 Olympics Gymnastics $1	225,173	182,676	81.13%	42,497	18.87%	0.750	30.02%	$37
1995 Olympics Paralympics	166,986	138,337	82.84%	28,649	17.16%	0.750	22.26%	$195
1995 Olympics Stadium $5	53,703	43,124	80.30%	10,579	19.70%	0.175	30.69%	$35
1995 Olympics Track and Field $1	161,731	136,935	84.67%	24,796	15.33%	0.750	21.56%	$33
1995 Special Olympics World Games	441,065	351,764	79.75%	89,301	20.25%	1.000	44.11%	$33
1996 Nat'l Community Service	125,043	101,543	81.21%	23,500	18.79%	0.500	25.01%	$37
1996 Olympic Swimming 50¢	163,848	114,315	69.77%	49,533	30.23%	3.000	5.46%	$33
1996 Olympics $5 Cauldron/ flame	47,765	38,555	80.72%	9,210	19.28%	0.300	15.92%	$31
1996 Olympics $5 Flag Bearers	42,060	32,886	78.19%	9,174	21.81%	0.300	14.02%	$31

Appendix: Mintages of U.S. Commemorative Coins

I. CHRONOLOGICAL GOLD AND SILVER COMMEMORATIVES (AND COPPER-NICKEL HALVES, TOO)								
	Minted	Proof	% Proof	Unc	% Unc	in Millions Authorized	Sold Percent	Selling price
1996 Olympics High Jump $1	140,199	124,502	88.80%	15,697	11.20%	1.000	14.02%	$31
1996 Olympics Rowing $1	168,148	151,890	90.33%	16,258	9.67%	1.000	16.81%	$13
1996 Olympics Soccer 50¢	175,248	122,412	69.85%	52,836	30.15%	2.000	8.76%	$33
1996 Olympics Tennis $1	107,999	92,016	85.20%	15,983	14.80%	1.000	10.80%	$31
1996 Paralympics Wheelchair	98,777	84,280	85.32%	14,497	14.68%	0.500	19.76%	$33
1996 Smithsonian 150th Anniv $5	30,840	21,772	70.60%	9,068	29.40%	0.100	30.84%	$13
1996 Smithsonian 150th Anniv.	160,382	129,152	80.53%	31,230	19.47%	0.650	24.67%	$37
1997 Franklin D. Roosevelt $5	41,368	29,474	71.25%	11,894	28.75%	0.100	41.37%	$205
1997 Jackie Robinson $1	140,502	110,495	78.64%	30,007	21.36%	0.200	70.25%	$10
1997 Jackie Robinson 50th Anniv	29,748	24,546	82.51%	5,202	17.49%	0.100	29.75%	$35

Appendix: Mintages of U.S. Commemorative Coins

I. CHRONOLOGICAL GOLD AND SILVER COMMEMORATIVES (AND COPPER-NICKEL HALVES, TOO)								
	Minted	Proof	% Proof	Unc	% Unc	in Millions Authorized	Sold Percent	Selling price
1997 National Law Enf. Mem.	139,003	110,428	79.44%	28,575	20.56%	0.500	27.80%	$31
1998 Black Patriots	112,280	75,070	66.86%	37,210	33.14%	0.500	22.46%	$28
1998 Black Patriots	112,280	75,070	66.86%	37,210	33.14%	0.500	22.46%	$28
1998 Robert F. Kennedy	205,442	99,020	48.20%	106,422	51.80%	0.500	41.09%	$28
1999 Dolley Madison $1	181,195	158,247	87.34%	22,948	12.66%	0.500	36.24%	$170
1999 George Washington	55,038	35,656	64.78%	19,382	35.22%	0.100	55.04%	$33
1999 Yellowstone $1	152,260	128,646	84.49%	23,614	15.51%	0.500	30.45%	$37
2000 Leif Erikson	86,762	58,612	67.55%	28,150	32.45%	0.500	17.35%	$10
2000 Library of Congress Gold/pt	33,850	27,167	80.26%	6,683	19.74%	0.200	16.93%	$10
2000 Library of Congress $1	249,671	196,900	78.86%	52,771	21.14%	0.500	49.93%	$352
2001 American Buffalo/ Indian	500,000	272,869	54.57%	227,131	45.43%	0.500	100.00%	$31
2001 Capitol Visitor Center	177,119	77,962	44.02%	99,157	55.98%	0.750	23.62%	$29

Appendix: Mintages of U.S. Commemorative Coins

I. CHRONOLOGICAL GOLD AND SILVER COMMEMORATIVES (AND COPPER-NICKEL HALVES, TOO)								
	Minted	Proof	% Proof	Unc	% Unc	in Millions Authorized	Sold Percent	Selling price
2001 Capitol Visitor Center	179,173	143,793	80.25%	35,380	19.75%	0.500	35.83%	$31
2001 Capitol Visitor Center	65,669	27,652	42.11%	38,017	57.89%	0.100	65.67%	$8
2002 Salt Lake City Olympics	42,523	32,351	76.08%	10,172	23.92%	0.080	53.15%	$28
2002 Salt Lake City Olympics $1	202,986	163,773	80.68%	39,213	19.32%	0.400	50.75%	$14
2002 West Point Military Bicentennial	363,852	267,184	73.43%	96,668	26.57%	0.500	72.77%	$10
2003 First Flight $10	31,975	21,846	68.32%	10,129	31.68%	0.100	31.98%	$28
2003 First Flight Centennial	169,295	111,569	65.90%	57,726	34.10%	0.750	0.00%	$200
2003 First Flight Centennial	246,847	193,086	78.22%	53,761	21.78%	0.500	49.37%	$28
2004 Edison	253,518	194,189	76.60%	59,329	23.40%	0.500	50.70%	$5
2004 Lewis & Clark	314,342	234,541	74.61%	79,801	25.39%	0.400	78.59%	$8
2005 Chief Justice Marshall	180,407	133,368	73.93%	47,039	26.07%	0.400	45.10%	$25

Appendix: Mintages of U.S. Commemorative Coins

I. CHRONOLOGICAL GOLD AND SILVER COMMEMORATIVES (AND COPPER-NICKEL HALVES, TOO)								
	Minted	Proof	% Proof	Unc	% Unc	in Millions Authorized	Sold Percent	Selling price
2005 Marines 230th Anniv.	500,000	370,000	74.00%	130,000	26.00%	0.600	83.33%	$25
2006 Ben Franklin 300 Youth	130,000	85,000	65.38%	45,000	34.62%	0.400	32.50%	$23
2006 Ben Franklin Old	130,000	85,000	65.38%	45,000	34.62%	0.400	32.50%	$14
2006 San Francisco	51,200	35,841	70.00%	15,359	30.00%	0.080	64.00%	$32
2006 San Francisco Mint	227,970	160,870	70.57%	67,100	29.43%	0.500	45.59%	$24
2007 Jamestown	60,805	43,609	71.72%	17,196	28.28%	0.080	76.01%	$10
2007 Jamestown 400th	289,880	213,065	73.50%	76,815	26.50%	0.500	57.98%	$22
2007 Little Rock	127,698	89,742	70.28%	37,956	29.72%	0.500	25.54%	$6
2008 Bald Eagle	340,974	248,688	72.93%	92,286	27.07%	0.500	68.19%	
2008 Bald Eagle $5	49,559	34,550	69.71%	15,009	30.29%	0.100	49.56%	
2008 Bald Eagle 50¢	293,599	195,858	66.71%	97,741	33.29%	0.750	39.15%	
2009 Abraham Lincoln Bicentennial	500,000	375,000	75.00%	125,000	25.00%	0.500	100.00%	
2009 Louis Braille	168,564	107,525	63.79%	61,039	36.21%	0.400	42.14%	31.95

Appendix: Mintages of U.S. Commemorative Coins

I. CHRONOLOGICAL GOLD AND SILVER COMMEMORATIVES (AND COPPER-NICKEL HALVES, TOO)								
	Minted	Proof	% Proof	Unc	% Unc	in Millions Authorized	Sold Percent	Selling price
2010 Am Vet Disabled for Life	267,410	189,551	70.88%	77,859	29.12%	0.350	76.40%	
2010 Boy Scouts	350,000	245,000	70.00%	105,000	30.00%	0.350	100.00%	33.95
2011 Medal of Honor	0					0.500		
2011 Medal of Honor	0					0.100		
2011 U.S. Army	0					0.750		
2011 U.S. Army	0					0.500		
2011 U.S. Army	0					0.100		
Averages			72.67%		24.55%			

2010 American Veterans Disabled for Life Commemorative Coin

Appendix: Mintages of U.S. Commemorative Coins

The commemorative coin chart sorted by mintage (column D, uncirculated) goes from low to high mintage. Uncirculateds are not as popular with collectors out of the box, but the low mintages affect their price substantially.

II. SORTED BY MINTAGE (HIGH-LOW UNCIRCULATED)								
	Minted	Proof	% Proof	Unc	% Unc	in Millions Authorized	Sold Percent	Selling price
1997 Jackie Robinson 50th Anniv	29,748	24,546	82.51%	5,202	17.49%	0.100	29.75%	$35
2000 Library of Congress gold/pt	33,850	27,167	80.26%	6,683	19.74%	0.200	16.93%	$10
1996 Smithsonian 150th Anniv $5	30,840	21,772	70.60%	9,068	29.40%	0.100	30.84%	$13
1996 Olympics $5 Flag Bearers	42,060	32,886	78.19%	9,174	21.81%	0.300	14.02%	$31
1996 Olympics $5 Cauldron/ Flame	47,765	38,555	80.72%	9,210	19.28%	0.300	15.92%	$31
2003 First Flight $10	31,975	21,846	68.32%	10,129	31.68%	0.100	31.98%	$28
2002 Salt Lake City Olympics	42,523	32,351	76.08%	10,172	23.92%	0.080	53.15%	$28
1995 Olympics Stadium $5	53,703	43,124	80.30%	10,579	19.70%	0.175	30.69%	$35
1997 Franklin D. Roosevelt $5	41,368	29,474	71.25%	11,894	28.75%	0.100	41.37%	$205
1995 Civil War Battle $5	67,981	55,246	81.27%	12,735	18.73%	0.300	22.66%	$12
1996 Paralympics Wheelchair	98,777	84,280	85.32%	14,497	14.68%	0.500	19.76%	$33

Appendix: Mintages of U.S. Commemorative Coins

II. SORTED BY MINTAGE (HIGH-LOW UNCIRCULATED)								
	Minted	Proof	% Proof	Unc	% Unc	in Millions Authorized	Sold Percent	Selling price
1995 Olympics $5 Runner	72,117	57,442	79.65%	14,675	20.35%	0.175	41.21%	$33
2008 Bald Eagle $5	49,559	34,550	69.71%	15,009	30.29%	0.100	49.56%	
2006 San Francisco	51,200	35,841	70.00%	15,359	30.00%	0.080	64.00%	$32
1996 Olympics High Jump $1	140,199	124,502	88.80%	15,697	11.20%	1.000	14.02%	$31
1996 Olympics Tennis $1	107,999	92,016	85.20%	15,983	14.80%	1.000	10.80%	$31
1996 Olympics Rowing $1	168,148	151,890	90.33%	16,258	9.67%	1.000	16.81%	$13
2007 Jamestown	60,805	43,609	71.72%	17,196	28.28%	0.080	76.01%	$10
1999 George Washington	55,038	35,656	64.78%	19,382	35.22%	0.100	55.04%	$33

2008 Bald Eagle Commemorative Coin

Appendix: Mintages of U.S. Commemorative Coins

II. SORTED BY MINTAGE (HIGH-LOW UNCIRCULATED)								
	Minted	Proof	% Proof	Unc	% Unc	in Millions Authorized	Sold Percent	Selling price
1995 Olympics cycling $1	138,457	118,795	85.80%	19,662	14.20%	0.750	18.46%	$37
1994 World Cup $5	112,066	89,614	79.97%	22,447	20.03%	5.000	2.24%	$37
1999 Dolley Madison $1	181,195	158,247	87.34%	22,948	12.66%	0.500	36.24%	$170
1993 Madison $5	101,928	78,654	77.17%	23,274	22.83%	0.300	33.98%	$33
1996 Nat'l Community Service	125,043	101,543	81.21%	23,500	18.79%	0.500	25.01%	$37
1994 WWII $5	90,434	66,837	73.91%	23,597	26.09%	0.300	30.14%	$35
1999 Yellowstone $1	152,260	128,646	84.49%	23,614	15.51%	0.500	30.45%	$37
1992 Columbus $5	104,065	79,734	76.62%	24,331	23.38%	0.500	20.81%	$195
1995 Olympics track and field $1	161,731	136,935	84.67%	24,796	15.33%	0.750	21.56%	$33
1992 Olympic $5	104,214	76,499	73.41%	27,715	26.59%	0.500	20.84%	$37
2000 Leif Erikson	86,762	58,612	67.55%	28,150	32.45%	0.500	17.35%	$10
1997 National Law Enf. Mem.	139,003	110,428	79.44%	28,575	20.56%	0.500	27.80%	$31

Appendix: Mintages of U.S. Commemorative Coins

II. SORTED BY MINTAGE (HIGH-LOW UNCIRCULATED)								
	Minted	Proof	% Proof	Unc	% Unc	in Millions Authorized	Sold Percent	Selling price
1995 Olympics Paralympics	166,986	138,337	82.84%	28,649	17.16%	0.750	22.26%	$195
1997 Jackie Robinson $1	140,502	110,495	78.64%	30,007	21.36%	0.200	70.25%	$10
1996 Smithsonian 150th Anniv.	160,382	129,152	80.53%	31,230	19.47%	0.650	24.67%	$37
1991 Mount Rushmore $5	143,950	111,991	77.80%	31,959	22.20%	0.500	28.79%	$35
2001 Capitol Visitor Center	179,173	143,793	80.25%	35,380	19.75%	0.500	35.83%	$31
1998 Black Patriots	112,280	75,070	66.86%	37,210	33.14%	0.500	22.46%	$28
1998 Black Patriots	112,280	75,070	66.86%	37,210	33.14%	0.500	22.46%	$28
2007 Little Rock	127,698	89,742	70.28%	37,956	29.72%	0.500	25.54%	$6
2001 Capitol Visitor Center	65,669	27,652	42.11%	38,017	57.89%	0.100	65.67%	$8
2002 Salt Lake City Olympics $1	202,986	163,773	80.68%	39,213	19.32%	0.400	50.75%	$14
1995 Olympics Gymnastics $1	225,173	182,676	81.13%	42,497	18.87%	0.750	30.02%	$37
2006 Ben Franklin 300 youth	130,000	85,000	65.38%	45,000	34.62%	0.400	32.50%	$23

Appendix: Mintages of U.S. Commemorative Coins

	Minted	Proof	% Proof	Unc	% Unc	in Millions Authorized	Sold Percent	Selling price
II. SORTED BY MINTAGE (HIGH-LOW UNCIRCULATED)								
2006 Ben Franklin old	130,000	85,000	65.38%	45,000	34.62%	0.400	32.50%	$14
1995 Civil War Battle $1	101,112	55,246	54.64%	45,866	45.36%	1.000	10.11%	
1989 CONG $5	211,589	164,690	77.83%	46,899	22.17%	1.000	21.16%	$225
2005 Chief Justice Marshall	180,407	133,368	73.93%	47,039	26.07%	0.400	45.10%	$25
1996 Olympic Swimming 50¢	163,848	114,315	69.77%	49,533	30.23%	3.000	5.46%	$33
1994 Women in Military	259,100	207,200	79.97%	51,900	20.03%	0.500	51.82%	$195
2000 Library of Congress $1	249,671	196,900	78.86%	52,771	21.14%	0.500	49.93%	$352
1996 Olympics Soccer 50¢	175,248	122,412	69.85%	52,836	30.15%	2.000	8.76%	$33
2003 First Flight Centennial	246,847	193,086	78.22%	53,761	21.78%	0.500	49.37%	$28
1994 P.O.W. $1	267,800	213,900	79.87%	53,900	20.13%	0.500	53.56%	$35
1994 Vietnam $1	275,800	219,300	79.51%	56,500	20.49%	0.500	55.16%	$37
2003 First Flight Centennial	169,295	111,569	65.90%	57,726	34.10%	0.750	0.00%	$200
2004 Edison	253,518	194,189	76.60%	59,329	23.40%	0.500	50.70%	$5

Appendix: Mintages of U.S. Commemorative Coins

II. SORTED BY MINTAGE (HIGH-LOW UNCIRCULATED)								
	Minted	Proof	% Proof	Unc	% Unc	in Millions Authorized	Sold Percent	Selling price
1994 Capitol Bicentennial $1	304,421	243,597	80.02%	60,824	19.98%	0.500	60.88%	$35
2009 Louis Braille	168,564	107,525	63.79%	61,039	36.21%	0.400	42.14%	31.95
2006 San Francisco Mint	227,970	160,870	70.57%	67,100	29.43%	0.500	45.59%	$24
1984 $10 Olympic Gold	573,364	497,478	86.76%	75,886	13.24%	1.000	57.34%	$350
2007 Jamestown 400th	289,880	213,065	73.50%	76,815	26.50%	0.500	57.98%	$22
2010 Am Vet Disabled for Life	267,410	189,551	70.88%	77,859	29.12%	0.350	76.40%	
2004 Lewis & Clark	314,342	234,541	74.61%	79,801	25.39%	0.400	78.59%	$8
1994 World Cup $1	656,567	577,090	87.73%	81,524	12.27%	5.000	13.13%	$37
1995 Special Olympics World Games	441,065	351,764	79.75%	89,301	20.25%	1.000	44.11%	$33
2008 Bald eagle	340,974	248,688	72.93%	92,286	27.07%	0.500	68.19%	
1986 Statue of Liberty $5	499,261	404,013	80.92%	95,248	19.08%	0.500	99.85%	$225
1993 Madison $1	627,995	532,747	84.83%	95,248	15.17%	0.900	69.78%	$33
2002 West Point Military Bicen	363,852	267,184	73.43%	96,668	26.57%	0.500	72.77%	$10

Appendix: Mintages of U.S. Commemorative Coins

II. SORTED BY MINTAGE (HIGH-LOW UNCIRCULATED)								
	Minted	Proof	% Proof	Unc	% Unc	in Millions Authorized	Sold Percent	Selling price
2008 bald eagle 50¢	293,599	195,858	66.71%	97,741	33.29%	0.750	39.15%	
2001 Capitol Visitor Center	177,119	77,962	44.02%	99,157	55.98%	0.750	23.62%	$29
2010 Boy Scouts	350,000	245,000	70.00%	105,000	30.00%	0.350	100.00%	33.95
1994 World War II $1	445,667	339,358	76.15%	106,309	23.85%	1.000	44.57%	$35
1998 Robert F. Kennedy	205,442	99,020	48.20%	106,422	51.80%	0.500	41.09%	$28
1992 Columbus $1	492,252	385,290	78.27%	106,962	21.73%	4.000	12.31%	$195
1995 Civil War 50¢	434,789	322,245	74.12%	112,544	25.88%	2.000	21.74%	$13
1992 White House $1	498,753	375,154	75.22%	123,599	24.78%	0.500	99.75%	$37
1991 USO $1	446,233	321,275	72.00%	124,958	28.00%	1.000	44.62%	$34
2009 Abraham Lincoln bicentennial	500,000	375,000	75.00%	125,000	25.00%	0.500	100.00%	
2005 Marines 230th anniv.	500,000	370,000	74.00%	130,000	26.00%	0.600	83.33%	$25
1988 Olympics $5	413,055	281,465	68.14%	131,590	31.86%	1.000	41.31%	$225
1991 Mount Rushmore $1	871,558	738,419	84.72%	133,139	15.28%	2.500	34.86%	$220

Appendix: Mintages of U.S. Commemorative Coins

II. SORTED BY MINTAGE (HIGH-LOW UNCIRCULATED)								
	Minted	Proof	% Proof	Unc	% Unc	in Millions Authorized	Sold Percent	Selling price
1989 Congress bicentennial 50 cent	897,401	762,198	84.93%	135,203	15.07%	4.000	22.44%	$225
1992 Columbus 50 cent	525,973	390,255	74.20%	135,718	25.80%	6.000	8.77%	$35
1992 Olympics 50 cent	678,484	517,318	76.25%	161,166	23.75%	6.000	11.31%	$37
1989 Congress $1	931,650	767,897	82.42%	163,753	17.58%	3.000	31.06%	$225
1995 Olympics Baseball 50¢	282,692	118,087	41.77%	164,605	58.23%	2.000	14.13%	$33
1994 World Cup 50	776,851	609,354	78.20%	168,208	21.80%	5.000	15.54%	$13
1995 Olympics Basketball 50¢	340,656	169,655	49.80%	171,001	50.20%	2.000	17.03%	$37

1989 Congress Bicentennial Half Dollar

Appendix: Mintages of U.S. Commemorative Coins

II. SORTED BY MINTAGE (HIGH-LOW UNCIRCULATED)								
	Minted	Proof	% Proof	Unc	% Unc	in Millions Authorized	Sold Percent	Selling price
1991 Mount Rushmore 50 cent	926,011	753,257	81.34%	172,754	18.66%	2.500	37.04%	$220
1992 Olympics $1	688,842	503,239	73.06%	185,603	26.94%	4.000	17.22%	$185
1993 Madison 50 Cent	775,287	584,350	75.37%	190,937	24.63%	1.000	77.53%	$33
1988 Olympics $1	1,550,734	1,359,366	87.66%	191,368	12.34%	10.000	15.51%	$259
1994 WWII 50 cent	512,759	313,801	61.20%	198,958	38.80%	2.000	25.64%	$35
1991 Korea $1	831,537	618,488	74.38%	213,049	25.62%	1.000	83.15%	$37
1987 Constitution $5	865,884	651,659	75.26%	214,225	24.74%	1.000	86.59%	$259
2001 American Buffalo/ Indian	500,000	272,869	54.57%	227,131	45.43%	0.500	100.00%	$31
1990 Eisenhower $1	1,386,130	1,144,461	82.57%	241,669	17.43%	4.000	34.65%	$259
1994 Jefferson	599,844	332,890	55.50%	266,954	44.50%	0.600	99.97%	$37
1984 Olympics $1	2,252,514	1,801,210	79.96%	451,304	20.04%	50.000	4.51%	$425
1987 Constitution $1	3,198,745	2,747,116	85.88%	451,629	14.12%	10.000	31.99%	$225
1983 Olympics $1	2,219,596	1,577,025	71.05%	642,571	28.95%	50.000	4.44%	$225

Appendix: Mintages of U.S. Commemorative Coins

II. SORTED BY MINTAGE (HIGH-LOW UNCIRCULATED)								
	Minted	Proof	% Proof	Unc	% Unc	in Millions Authorized	Sold Percent	Selling price
1986 Statue of Liberty $1	7,138,273	6,414,638	89.86%	723,635	10.14%	10.000	71.38%	$225
1986 Statue of Liberty 50 C	7,853,635	6,925,627	88.18%	928,008	11.82%	10.000	78.54%	$259
1982 Washington 50 cent	7,104,502	4,894,044	68.89%	2,210,458	31.11%	10.000	71.05%	$225
2011 Medal of Honor	0					0.500	0.00%	
2011 Medal of Honor	0					0.100	0.00%	
2011 U.S. Army	0					0.750	0.00%	
2011 U.S. Army	0					0.500	0.00%	
2011 U.S. Army	0					0.100	0.00%	
Averages			74.25%		25.26%		38.29%	

Statue of Liberty Half Dollar

Selected Bibliography

Adams, E.A. and W.H. Woodin. *United States Pattern, Trial and Experimental Pieces.* 1913, reprinted 1940.

Carothers, *N. Fractional Money.* 1930.

The Congressional Record, various issues 1994-1996.

CPM Gold Yearbook 2006-2011.

CPM Platinum Yearbook 2006-2009.

CPM Silver Yearbook 2006-2009.

Craf, J.R. *Economic Development of the U.S.* McGraw Hill, 1952.

Dodd, D. *Historical Statistics of the States of the U.S., 1790-1990.* Greenwood Publishers, 1993.

Edwards Metcalfe collection (platinum). Superior Stamp & Coin.

Friedman, M. and A. Schwartz. *A Monetary History of the U.S. 1867-1960.* National Bureau of Economic Research. 1963.

Ganz, D.L. "The Age of Gold." *The Numismatist*, 1973.

Ganz, D.L. "The Coinage Act of 1873 and the Denominatization of Silver." *The Numismatist*, 1973.

Geisst, Charles R. *Wall Street: A History.* Oxford U. Press, 1997.

The Gold Institute. *Modern Gold Coinage.* 1995.

Hamilton, A. "Report on the Mint." *Papers of Alexander Hamilton vol. 7.* ed. Syrett. 1963.

The Harold S Bareford collection of U.S. Gold Coins. Stack's auction catalog, Dec. 12, 1978.

Harry Bass Foundation website. http://www.hbrf.org/

Hepburn, A. Barton. *History of Coinage & Currency of the U.S.* 1903, reprinted 1968.

Heritage Numismatic Auctions. Various catalogs and website. http://www.ha.com.

Jefferson, T. *Notes on Coinage.* 1786.

The John Jay Pittman collection (auction by David W. Akers), vols 1-3. 1997-1999.

Judd, W.H. *United States Pattern, Experimental & Trial Pieces, 6th ed.* 1977.

Long, K.R., J. H. DeYoung, Jr., and S. D. Ludington. U.S. Department of the Interior U.S. Geological Survey Database of Significant Deposits of Gold, Silver, Copper, Lead, and Zinc In the United States Part A: Database Description and Analysis, Open-File Report 98-206A. 1998.

Matthey, J. Platinum 1996: Interim Review. November 1996.

Minerals Yearbooks 1937-2011. U.S. Geological Survey

Murphy, J. "Has U.S. $5 Coin Struck in Platinum," *The Numismatist,* 1939.

BIBLIOGRAPHY

Parker, N. French platinum. *Coins* vol.10, April 1963.

Parker, N. German platinum. *Coins* vol.10, May 1963.

Parker, N. International platinum. *Coins* vol.11, April 1964.

Parker, N. Russian platinum. *Coins* vol.11, May 1964.

Parker, N. Spanish platinum. *Coins* vol.10, February 1963.

Parker, N. U.S. Platinum coinage. *Coins* vol.11, February 1964.

Pollock, A. *United States Patterns & Related Issues.* 1994.

Public Law 104-208. Approved September 30, 1996.

ScotiaMocatta. http://www.scotiamocatta.com/products/glossary.htmhd

Simon, J., ed. *Papers of Ulysses S. Grant July 1, 1868-Oct. 31, 1868, vol. 19.* 1995.

Snowden, J.R. *A Description of Ancient and Modern coins in the Cabinet of the United States.* 1859.

US Geological Survey, Minerals, Palladium; US Geological Survey, Minerals, for Gold, Silver, Platinum.

Various. *Annual Report of the Director of the Mint.* 1792-date (U.S. Gov't publication).

Waugh, J. *U.S. Grant, American Hero, American Myth.* 2009.

Whitman Publishing. *Precious Metals.* 2011.